The Story of the Alphabet

Edward Clodd

Alpha Editions

This edition published in 2024

ISBN : 9789362994806

Design and Setting By
Alpha Editions
www.alphaedis.com
Email - info@alphaedis.com

Contents

PREFACE

If this little book does not supply a want, it fills, however imperfectly, a gap; for the only work in the English language on the subject—Canon Isaac Taylor's "History of the Alphabet"—is necessarily charged with a mass of technical detail which is stiff reading even for the student of graphiology. Moreover, invaluable and indispensable as is that work, it furnishes only a meagre account of those primitive stages of the art of writing, knowledge of which is essential for tracing the development of that art, so that its place in the general evolution of human inventions is made clear. Prominence is therefore given to this branch of the subject in the following pages.

In the recent reprint of Canon Taylor's book no reference occurs to the important materials collected by Professor Flinders Petrie and Mr. Arthur J. Evans in Egypt and Crete, the result of which is to revolutionise the old theory of the source of the Alphabet whence our own and others are derived. This opens up a big question for experts to settle; and here it must suffice to present a statement of the new evidence, and to point out its significance, so that the reader be not taken into the troubled atmosphere of controversy. That he may, further, not be distracted by footnotes, references to the authorities cited are printed in the text.

E. C.

ROSEMONT, 19 CARLETON ROAD,
Tufnell Park, N

CHAPTER I
INTRODUCTORY

"What is ever seen is never seen," and it may be questioned if one in ten thousand of the readers of to-day ever pauses to ask what is the history of the conventional signs called the ALPHABET, which, in their varying changes of position, make up the symbols of the hundred thousand words and more contained in a comprehensive dictionary of the English tongue.

Professor Max Müller says that "by putting together twenty-three or twenty-four letters in every possible variety. We might produce every word that has ever been used in any language of the world. The number of these words, taking twenty-three letters as the basis, would be **25,852,016,738,884,976,640,000**, or, if we took twenty-four, would be **620,448,401,733,239,439,360,000**; but," as the Professor warns us, in words the force of which will be manifest later on, "even these trillions, billions, and millions of sounds would not be words, because they would lack the most important ingredient—that which makes a word to be a word—namely, the different ideas by which they were called into life, and which are expressed differently in different languages." (Lectures on Language, ii. 81.)

These words themselves, as will also be shown concerning the ear-pictures by which they are represented, reveal in their analysis a story of the deepest interest. In the happy simile quoted by the late Archbishop Trench in his Study of Words, they are "fossil history," and, as he adds, "fossil poetry and fossil ethics" also. To cite a few examples, more or less apposite to our subject, "book" is probably from the Anglo-Saxon bóc, a "beech," tablets of the bark of that tree being one of the substances on which written characters were inscribed. Parallel to this are the words "library" and "libel," both derived from the Latin liber, the inner bark or rind of a tree used for paper; while, as everybody knows, the word "paper" preserves the history of the manufacture of writing material in Egypt from the pith of the papyrus reed, the use of which goes back, as will be shown hereafter, to a high antiquity, and the classic name of which, biblos, has been applied to "bible." "Code" is derived from the Latin codex, "a tree-trunk"; "letters" comes through the French lettre from the Latin lino, litum, "to daub" or "besmear," an early mode of writing being the graving of characters on tablets smeared with wax. "Tablet" is the diminutive of "table," which comes from the Latin tabula, "a board," and the ancient writing instrument, called a stylus, illustrates the passage of language from the concrete to the abstract in its application to the way in which a writer expresses his ideas.

We speak of his "style," just as we say "he wields an able pen," this word being derived from the Latin penna, "a feather." The phrase lapsus calami, "a slip of the pen," preserves record of the use of the reed (Latin calamus), which also survives in "quill," from Old English quylle, "a reed." But the metal pen has a longer history than was suspected, since Dr. Waldstein has found one, cut and slit like our modern specimens, in a tomb of the third century B.C., at Eretria in the island of Eubœa in the Ægean. "Volume," from Latin volumen, "a roll," tells us what was the usual form of books in ancient times, the old form of preservation and custody of legal records surviving in "Rolls of Court," "Master of the Rolls," and so forth. So in "diploma," which, literally, is a paper folded double, from Greek diploō, "to fold." Both "diplomacy" and "duplicity" mean "doubling," but the force of the parallel may not be pursued here. Finally—for the list might be extended indefinitely—"parchment" is borrowed from Pergamus, a town in Asia Minor, where skin came into general use, Ptolemy V. (205-185 B.C.), so runs a doubtful story told by Pliny, having prohibited the export of papyrus from Egypt.

As words, under the analyses now indicated, yield the history of their origin and of the changes both in spelling and meaning which follow their passage from older forms, and likewise reveal the reasons which governed the choice of them, so the letters of which they are made up bear witness to similar laws of development. The story which it is the purpose of this little book to endeavour to extract from them has mutilated and imperfect chapters, and, moreover, missing chapters which may never be recovered. But sufficing material survives for piecing together a narrative of the triumph of the human mind over one of the most difficult tasks to which it could apply itself; a task which, unwrought, would have made advance in the highest sense impossible beyond a certain point. In the highest sense, because man has gone a long way without knowledge either of reading or writing. These "two R's" are not necessary in matters of personal contact with his fellows, while in other ways progress is independent of them. An illiterate man may be an accomplished landscape artist, a skilful engineer, a successful farmer or trader, and prosperous in many ways where the aim of life is to "live by bread alone." It is true that much of the intellectual and spiritual record of man's past was long preserved in the form of oral tradition. But to the volume of such record there is a limit, while time and caprice alike work havoc in it. Memory, great as was its capacity of old, before dependence on books impaired it, was not infallible, nor, as the world's stock of knowledge increased, could it "pull down its barns and build greater wherein to bestow its goods." We have, by an effort of the imagination well-nigh impossible to make, only to assume the absence of any means of material record of the involved and myriad events which fill the world's past, to conceive the intellectual poverty of the present. We have only to assume the absence of any medium whereby we could communicate with friends at a distance, or whereby the now complex and countless dealings between man and man could be set down and every transaction thus "brought to book," to realise the hopeless tangle of our social life. All that memory failed to overlap would be an absolute blank; the dateless and otherwise uninscribed monuments which the past had left behind would but deepen the darkness; all knowledge of the strivings and speculations of men of old would have been unattainable; all observation and experience through which science has advanced from guesses to certainties irretrievably lost; life could have been lived only from "hand to mouth," and the spectacle presented of an arrested world of sentient beings. Save in fragmentary echoes repeated by fugitive bards, the great epics of East and West would have perished, and the immortal literatures of successive ages never have existed. The invention of writing alone made possible the passage from barbarism to civilisation, and secured the continuous progress of the human race. It is solely through the marvellous perfecting, through stages of slow advance, of a scripture that "cannot be broken," that the past is as eloquent, as real, as the present. "The pen is mightier than the sword" in accumulating and preserving for both gentle and simple the store of the world's intellectual wealth, unto which "all the things that can be desired are not to be compared."

These reflections are commonplace enough, but they may not be wholly needless, and an example or two of the impression made on the barbaric mind by written symbols may help us the better to appreciate what our case would be without them. In the narrative of his adventures in the Tonga Islands, published about ninety years ago, William Mariner tells how anxiety to escape from the place where, on the wreck of the ship Port au Prince, he and some other Englishmen had been cast ashore, led him to write, by means of a solution of gunpowder and a little mucilage for ink, a letter which he entrusted to a friendly native to give to the captain of any vessel that might happen to touch at Tonga. Finow, the king, came to hear of this, and got hold of the letter. But he could make "neither head nor tail" of it. However, by threats of death if he refused, one of Mariner's shipmates was made to interpret the mystic signs to Finow, who, still puzzled, sent for Mariner and ordered him to write down something else, saying, when Mariner asked for a subject, "Put down me." This done, Finow sent for another sailor, who read the royal name aloud, whereupon the king appeared more bewildered than ever, exclaiming. "This not like me; where are my legs?" Then it slowly dawned upon him that it was possible to make signs of things which both the writer and the interpreter had seen. But the bewilderment returned when Mariner told him that he could write down a description of any one whom he had never seen, or of an event which happened long ago or far away, when these were told him. Thereupon

Finow whispered to him the name of Tongoo Aho, a former king of Tonga, who, it had come to Mariner's knowledge, was blind in one eye. When Mariner set these things down, and the king had them read to him, it was explained that "in several parts of the world messages were sent to great distances through the same medium, and, being folded and fastened up, the bearer could know nothing of the contents; and that the histories of whole nations were thus handed down to posterity without spoiling by being kept. Finow acknowledged this to be a most noble invention, but added that it would not at all do for the Tonga Islands; that there would be nothing but disturbances and conspiracies, and he should not be sure of his life perhaps another month. He said, however, jocularly, that he should like to know it himself, and for all the women to know it, that he might make love with less risk of discovery, and not so much chance of incurring the vengeance of their husbands." (Mariner's Tonga Islands, i. 116, ed. 1827.) The Smithsonian Reports, 1864, tell a story of an Indian who was sent by a missionary to a colleague with four loaves of bread, accompanied by a letter stating their number. The Indian ate one of the loaves, and was, of course, found out. He was sent on a similar errand and repeated the theft, but took the precaution to hide the letter under a stone while he was eating the bread, so that it might not see him!

Barbaric ideas fall into fundamentally-related groups, and the examples just given are connected with the widespread belief in the efficacy of written characters to work black or white magic, to effect cures, and otherwise act as charms—a belief largely derived from the legends which ascribe the origin of writing to the gods—legends themselves the product of Ignorance, the mother of Mystery. In an Assyrian inscription, Sardanapalus V. speaks of the cuneiform or wedge-shaped characters as a revelation to his royal ancestors from the god Nebo; among the Egyptians, Thoth was the scribe of the gods, and their oldest forms of writing were named "the divine." Chinese tradition ascribes the invention of writing to the dragon-faced, four-eyed sage Ts'ang Chien, who saw in the stars of heaven, the footprints of birds, and the marks on the back of the tortoise, the models on which he formed the written characters. At this invention "heaven caused showers of grain to descend from on high; the disembodied spirits wept in the darkness, and the dragons withdrew themselves from sight." On the altars raised to Ts'ang Chien throughout the Celestial Land, every scrap of fugitive paper which has writing on it is burned in his honour. In Hindu legend, Brahma, the supreme god of the Indian Trinity, gives knowledge of letters to men; and Nâgari, in which alphabet the sacred books are written, is spoken of as "belonging to the city of the gods." The handwriting of Brahma, legend further says, is seen in the serrated sutures of men's skulls; and as Yahweh or Jehovah wrote the "Ten Words" with his own finger, so Brahma inscribed the holy texts of the Veda on leaves of gold. The story of the culture-hero, Cadmus, introducing the alphabet from Phœnicia into Greece is well known; while in Irish legend, Ogmios, the Gaelish Hercules, is familiar as the inventor of writing. But perhaps less familiar is that in the Northern Saga which attributes the invention of runes to Odin:—

"Thought-runes shalt thou deal with If thou wilt be of all men Fairest-souled, wight and wisest. These are ded, These first cut, These first took to heart high Hropt." (Odin.)

Belief in the power of the spoken word, notably as a curse, has world-wide illustration; and not less is that in the power of the written word or of the pictorial symbol. Cabalistic formulæ and texts from sacred writings play a large part; the virtue in Jewish phylacteries and frontlets was believed to depend on the texts which they enclosed; the amulets worn by Abyssinians to avert the evil eye and ward off demons have the secret name of God chased on them; passages from the Koran are enclosed in bags and hung on Turkish and Arab horses to protect them against like maleficence; prayers to the Madonna are slipped into charm-cases to be worn by the Neapolitans; while not so many years back (indeed, so persistent are superstitions, that kindred practices obtain throughout Europe to this day) sick folk in the Highlands were fanned with the leaves of the Bible.

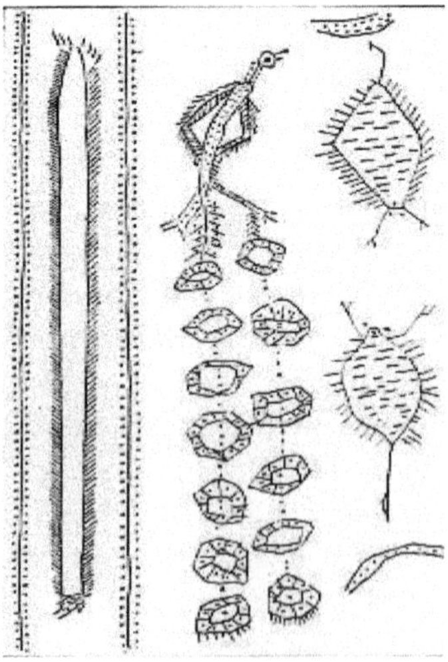

Fig. 1.—Magical Pictograph against Stings

In his instructive and entertaining book on Evolution in Art, Professor Haddon refers to a series of valuable observations on the use of picture-writing as a charm against diseases and stings of venomous animals, among the Semang tribes of East Malacca, made by Mr. H. Vaughan Stevens, and edited by Mr. A. Grünwedel. The women wear bamboo combs on which are drawn patterns of flowers or parts of flowers believed to be antidotes to fevers and other invisible diseases; for injuries and wounds such as those caused by a falling bough in the jungle, or the bite of a centipede, other means are employed. Among the magic-working devices incised in bamboo staves by the Semang magicians, Mr. Vaughan Stevens gives illustrations of one against the stings of scorpions and centipedes (Fig. 1), and of another against a skin disease (Fig. 2).

In the first-named there is depicted the figure of an Argus pheasant, the wheel-like patterns beneath which represent the eye-marks in the tail-feathers. On the left is an orange-coloured centipede, the head of which points to the tail of the pheasant. The dotted lines round the centipede are tracks which it leaves on a man's skin. On the other side of the Argus are two blue scorpions, the figures at the end of their tails representing a swelling in the flesh of the persons stung by them. The female of this kind of scorpion is more poisonous than the male, and is said to cause double stings, which are denoted by the two rows of dots in the top figure. "The significance of this bamboo is that as the Argus pheasant feeds on centipedes and scorpions, so its help is invoked against them by striking the bamboo against the ground."

Fig. 2.—Magical Device against Skin Disease

The other example, which exhibits a much more complicated and conventionalised device, is designed as a charm against two kinds of skin disease, the one represented by fish scales indicating leprous white ulcers, the other represented by oval figures indicating hard knots on and under the skin. The rows stand for the several parts of the body which are affected, and the figures increase in size to show that the disease will spread if not cured. Although the way in which the charm is applied is not clear, there is no doubt that belief in its virtue belongs to the large class of barbaric ideas grouped under sympathetic magic, i.e. that things outwardly resembling one another are thought by the barbaric or illiterate to possess the same qualities. The result is that effects are brought about in the individual himself by the production of similar effects in things belonging to him, or, what is more to the purpose, in images or effigies of him. Here it suffices to say that the most familiar examples of "sympathetic magic" are the making of an image of the person whose destruction is sought, of wax, clay, or other substance, so that as the wax is melted, or the clay dissolved in running water, his life may decline or wear away to its doom. Such examples are gathered alike from civilised and barbaric folk, from Devonshire and the Highlands to North America and Borneo.

Things are invested with mystery in the degree that their origins and causes are unknown; and the beliefs and customs, of which a few among the teeming illustrations have been given, invite the reflection that, had writing remained the monopoly of any caste or class, it would have remained an engine of enslavement, instead of becoming an engine of liberation of the mind. "Knowledge is power," and whatever has ensured the possession and the retention of power over his fellows has been seized upon by man—notably by man as priest, from medicine-man to Pope, as wielder of weapons of authority, the more dreaded when unseen or intangible. Signs which were unadapted, and, things being what they then were, impossible, for general use, and moreover needing great expenditure of time and labour to master them, would come under this head, and it was only through their ultimate simplification that they could become serviceable to the many, and made vehicles of the diffusion of knowledge. How monstrous and penal an instrument of inequality learning itself long continued among ourselves is shown in the fact that "benefit of clergy"—one among many evidences of the old conflict between the civil and the sacerdotal powers—was not wholly repealed until the year 1827. Under this statute, exemption from trial for criminal offences before secular courts was extended, by law passed in the reign of Edward I., not only to ecclesiastics, but to any man who could read. A prisoner sentenced to death might be claimed by the bishop of the diocese as a clerk and haled before him, when the ordinary gave the man a Latin book from which to read a verse or two. If the ordinary said "Legit ut clericus"—i.e. "he reads like a clerk"—the offender was only burnt in the hand, and then set free.

CHAPTER II
THE BEGINNINGS OF THE ALPHABET

We may, without further preface, advance to our main purpose, which is to supply an account of the stages through which the alphabets of the civilised world passed before they reached their, practically, final form. Here, as in aught else that the wit of man has devised and the cunning of his hand applied, the law of development is seen at work. In the quest for traces of any fundamental differences between him and the animals to which he stands in nearest physical and psychical relation, he has been variously described as tool-maker, fire-maker, possessor of articulate speech, and so forth; but the further that observation and comparison have been made, the more apparent has it become that those differences are of degree and not of kind. Some evidence in support of this has been already summarised in previous volumes of this series; and here it suffices to say that it is in the inventive arts, as e.g. the production of fire, of the mode of which nature supplied the hints, and the making of pictorial signs, in which the mimetic instinct, shared by some of the lower animals, comes into play, that, restricting the comparison to things material, man appears upon a higher plane. But this has been reached by processes of development involving no break in the continuity of things.

In this "story" we start with man as sign-maker. His prehistoric remains supply evidence of artistic capacity in a remote past, and set before us in vigorous, rapid outline what his life and surroundings must have been. On fragments of bone, horn, schist, and other materials, the savage hunter of the Reindeer Period, using a pointed flint flake, depicted alike himself and the wild animals which he pursued. From cavern-floors of France, Belgium, and other parts of Western Europe, whose deposits date from the old Stone Age, there have been unearthed rude etchings of naked, hardy men brandishing spears at wild horses, or creeping along the ground to hurl their weapons at the urus, or wild ox, or at the woolly-haired elephant. A portrait of this last named, showing the creature's shaggy ears, long hair, and upwardly curved tusks, its feet being hidden in the surrounding high grass, is one of the most famous examples of palæolithic art.

Here let us pause to say that the apparent absence of other indications of man's presence, showing passage from lower to higher stages of culture, led to the assumption that vast gaps have occurred in his occupancy of north-western and other parts of Europe. The theory of absolute disconnection between the Old Stone Age and the Newer Stone Age long held the field, but it has disappeared before the evidence against tenantless intervals of areas in prehistoric times. And so with succeeding periods. There is no warrant for assuming entire effacement of one race, with resulting clear field for the immigration of another race; and modern archæological research is producing the links which connect the rude art of Northern with that of Southern Europe, and, what will be shown to be of great moment, with that of the Eastern Mediterranean. The examples of this must remain rare, since only pictographs on some durable material, or specimens of the fictile art, would survive the action of time. But, happily, if they are infrequent, they are widely distributed. For to those yielded by the bone-caverns already referred to are to be added rock-carvings in Denmark, and figures on limestone cliffs of the Maritime Alps; there are curious graphic signs, suggestive to some eyes of a primitive script, in the Marz d'Azil cave; while still more interesting are the animal and fylfot or swastika-like figures (the swastika is a solar symbol) "painted probably by early Slavonic hands on the face of a rock overhanging a sacred grotto in a fiord of the Bocche di Cattaro." To this last-named example, given by Mr. Arthur Evans in his paper on "Primitive Pictographs" (Journal of Hellenic Studies, xiv. ii. 1894) may be added some pregnant remarks by the same authority. "When we recall the spontaneous artistic qualities of the ancient race which has left its records in the carvings on bone and ivory in the caves of the 'Reindeer Period,' this evidence of at least partial continuity on the northern shores of the Mediterranean suggests speculations of the deepest interest. Overlaid with new elements, swamped in the dull, though materially higher, Neolithic civilisation, may not the old æsthetic faculties which made Europe the earliest-known home of anything that can be called human art, as opposed to mere tools and mechanical contrivances, have finally emancipated themselves once more in the Southern regions, where the old stock most survived? In the extraordinary manifestations of artistic genius to which, at widely remote periods and under the most diverse political conditions, the later populations of Greece and Italy have given birth, may we not be allowed to trace the re-emergence, as it were, after long underground meanderings, of streams whose upper waters had seen the daylight of that earlier world?" (Presidential Address to the Anthropological Section, British Association. Nature, 1st Oct. 1896.)

But man at the same stage of culture being everywhere practically the same, there is, in the paucity of examples from the Europe of the past, compensation in the specimens of graphic art found among extant barbaric folk. It is probable that a good proportion of these lack significance, but the pictograph is the parent of the alphabet, and therefore the careful transcripts of rock and other paintings which explorers have made may yet prove to be of value when interpreted in the light of examples whose gradations have been traced. Since the extinction of the Tasmanians, whom anthropologists regard as the nearest approach to Palæolithic man, the

Australians stand, in certain respects, at the bottom of the scale, although the ingenuity of their social organisations warrants hesitation in making them the nadir of human kind. But as the reproductions show (Figs. 3 and 3a), their attempts at art are inferior to the spirited designs of the prehistoric cave-dwellers.

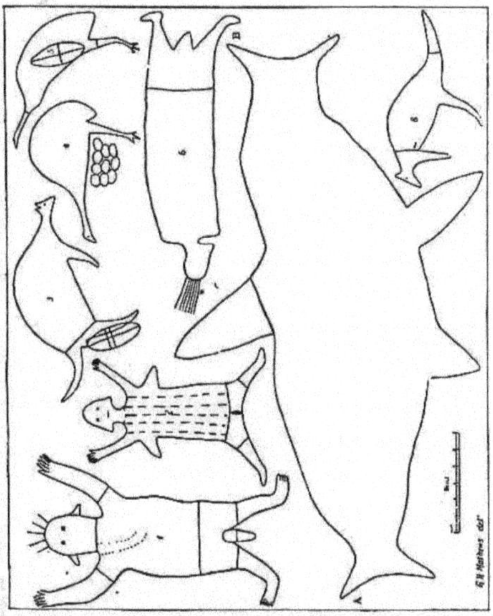

Fig. 3.—Aboriginal Rock Carvings (Australia)

Fig. 3a.—Aboriginal Rock Paintings (Australia)

Mr. R. H. Mathews, who has made an extensive survey of the rock-paintings and carvings, says that one type serves for another, so lacking are all in variety; "the stencilled and impressed hands, the outlines of men and animals rudely depicted in various colours, appearing to be universally distributed over the continent." He adds that "although it will be better not to attempt to suggest meanings to the groups of native drawings until a very much larger amount of information has been brought together ... still when we know that drawings such as these by uncivilised nations of all times, in various parts of the world, have ultimately been found to be full of meaning, it is not unreasonable for us to expect that the strange figures painted and carved upon rocks all over Australia will some day be interpreted. Perhaps some of these pictures are ideographic expressions of events in the history of the tribe; certain groupings of figures may portray some legend; many of the animals probably represent totems; and it is likely that a number of them were executed for pastime and amusement." (Journal of the Anthropological Institute, xxv. 2, p. 153.) In their recently published "Native Tribes of Central Australia," Messrs. Spencer and Gillen divide the rock-paintings into two series, those of ordinary type, and those which, found in places strictly taboo to women and children and uninitiated men, are associated with totems, i.e. with the natural object, whether living or non-living, from which the tribe believes itself to be descended. These totemistic figures, called Churinga (a general native term for sacred objects) Ilkinia, are frequently in the form of spiral and concentric circles, others being portraits of the totems themselves, as low in type as the centipede or witchetty grub.

Fig. 4.—Bushman Paintings

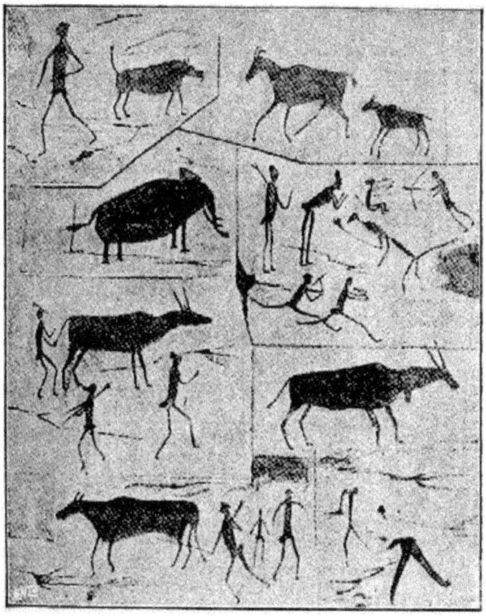

Fig. 4a.—Bushman Paintings

The faces of sandstone caverns in South Africa are often covered with paintings which are the handiwork of Bushmen (Figs. 4, 4a, and 4b). With a skill showing some advance on the art of the Australian aborigines there is depicted, usually in black or brownish-red colour, the hunting and other exploits which make up life among a people who represent the aboriginal races of the southern portion of the continent. Some of the drawings border on caricature; others, in the words of an observer, "suggest actual portraiture. The ornamentation of the head-dresses, feathers, beads tassels, &c., seemed to have claimed much care, while the higher class of drawings indicate correct appreciation of the actual appearance of objects, and perspective and foreshortening are well rendered." (Mark Hutchinson, Journal of the Anthropological Institute, xiv. p. 464.)

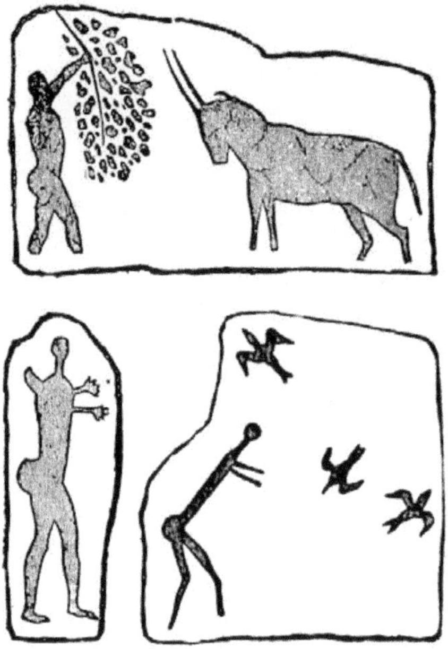

Fig. 4b.—Specimen of Bushmen Rock Sculptures

Fig. 4c.—Engravings found on Rocks in Algeria

(compare with Bushmen type)

These probably now degraded folk, who live on lizards, locusts, and roots when other food fails, have a good store of legend and folk-lore. Fig. 5 seems to portray their belief in "sympathetic magic," if, as conjectured, it represents the dragging of an hippopotamus or other amphibious animal across the land for the purpose of producing rain. The Semangs of the Malay Peninsula use a bamboo rain-charm (Fig. 6), on which the wind-driven showers are depicted in oblique lines, and, among many other examples wherein the higher and lower culture meet together, there is one supplied by old Rome, where it was the custom to throw images of the corn-spirit into the Tiber so that the crops might be drenched with rain. As showing the persistency of superstitions, here is a paragraph anent the severe drought in Russia last autumn: "In another village of the district of Bugulma some moujiks opened the grave of a peasant who had lately been buried, and then poured water over the corpse, in the belief that this was the best method of bringing rain."—Daily Chronicle, 24th August 1899.

Fig. 5.—Bushman Rain-Charm.

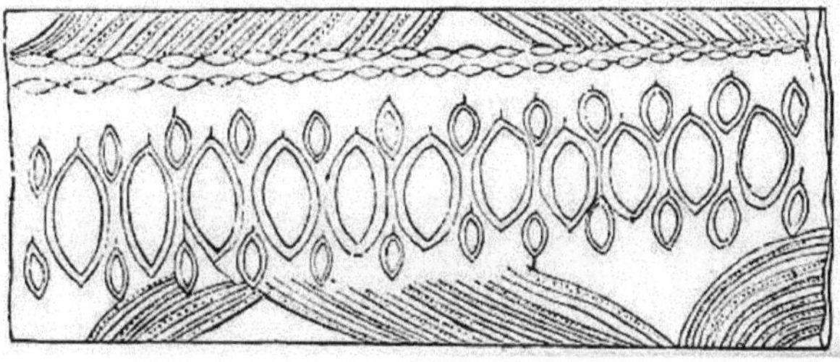

Fig. 6.—Semang Rain-Charm.

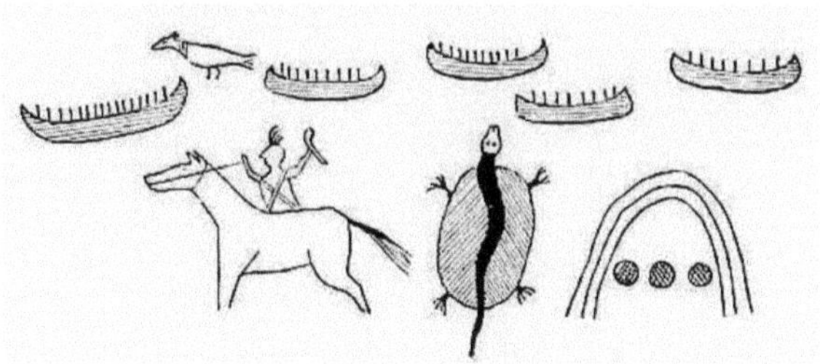

Fig. 6a.—Record of Expedition.

The New World is rich in ancient monuments often adorned with symbolic devices, but older than these are the pictographs covering erratic blocks and cliff escarpments from Guiana to Nova Scotia, and westward to the Rockies. Some are incised in the hard stone to a depth of half an inch; others are traced in broad lines of red ochre or other colour, their weather-worn state witnessing to a high antiquity. Their purpose is often not easy to explain, but we know that therein lie the germs whence alphabets sprung. One picture (Fig. 6a) on the face of a rock on the shore of Lake Superior, copied and interpreted by Schoolcraft, records an expedition across the lake, led by Myeengun, or "Wolf," a noted Indian chief. The crew of each canoe is denoted by a series of upright strokes, Myeengun's chief ally, Kishkemanusee, the "Kingfisher," being in the first canoe. The arch with three circles (three suns under heaven) shows that the voyage took three days. The tortoise (a frequent symbol of "land" in North American picture-writing) seems to indicate the arrival of the expedition, while the picture of the mounted chief evidences that the event took place after the introduction of horses into Canada. Some of the examples, less easy to explain, represent the migration of tribes; some, like the sculptured eagle near the borders of Quauhuahuac ("the place near the eagle") are symbolic boundary-marks; while others are direction-marks. Some have life-size human figures, rayed or horned; one engraved on a rock overlooking the Big Harpeth, in Tennessee, depicts a sun visible four miles off. Doubtless a large number of this class (Fig. 6b) are merely the outcome of that rude artistic fancy of man which, as has been seen, has had continuous expression from prehistoric times.

Fig. 6b.—Various Types of the Human Form

CHAPTER III
MEMORY-AIDS AND PICTURE-WRITING

The printed letters or sound-signs which compose our alphabet are about two thousand five hundred years old. "Roman type" we call them, and rightly so, since from Italy they came. They vary only in slight degree from the founts of the famous printers of the fifteenth century, these being imitations of the beautiful "minuscule" (so called as being of smaller size) manuscripts of four hundred years earlier. Minuscule letters are cursive (i.e. running) forms of the curved letters about an inch long called "uncials" (from Latin uncia, "an inch," or from uncus, "crooked"), which were themselves derived from the Roman letters of the Augustan age. These Roman capitals, to which those in modern use among us correspond, "are practically identical with the letters employed at Rome in the third century B.C.; such, for instance, as are seen in the well-known inscriptions on the tombs of the Scipios, now among the treasures of the Vatican. These, again, do not differ very materially from forms used in the earliest existing specimens of Latin writing, which may probably be referred to the end of the fifth century B.C. Thus it appears that our English alphabet is a member of that great Latin family of alphabets, whose geographical extension was originally conterminous, or nearly so, with the limits of the Western Empire, and afterwards with the ancient obedience to the Roman See." (Canon Isaac Taylor's History of the Alphabet, vol. i. p. 71.)

The age of our own alphabet being thus indicated, we may postpone further remark on its lineal descent, and pass to inquiry into the primitive forms of which all alphabets are the abbreviated descendants, and also to reference to some primitive methods for which they are substitutes.

A survey of the long period which this development covers shows four well-marked stages, although in these, as in aught else appertaining to man's history, there are no true lines of division. The making of these, like the apparent lines of longitude and latitude of the cartographer, is justified by their convenience. These stages are:—

(a) **The MNEMONIC**, or memory-aiding, when some tangible object is used as a message, or for record, between people at a distance, and also for the purpose of accrediting the messenger. As will be seen, it borders on the symbolic; indeed, it anticipates that stage.

(b) **The PICTORIAL**, in which a picture of the thing is given, whereby at a glance it tells its own story.

(c) **The IDEOGRAPHIC**, in which the picture becomes representative, i.e. is converted into a symbol.

(d) **The PHONETIC**, in which the picture becomes a phonogram, or sound-representing sign. The phonogram may be—(1) verbal, i.e. a sound-sign for a whole word; (2) syllabic, i.e. a sound-sign for syllables; or (3) alphabetic, a sound-sign for each letter.

To recapitulate stages (b), (c), and (d):—

In stage (b) the sign as eye-picture suggests the thing;

In stage (c) the sign as eye-picture suggests the name;

In stage (d) the sign as ear-picture suggests the sound;

and it is in the passage from (c) to (d), whereby constant signs are chosen to stand for constant sounds, that the progress of the human race was assured, because only thereby was the preservation of all that is of abiding value made possible.

Fig. 7.—Quipu, for Reckoning, &c.

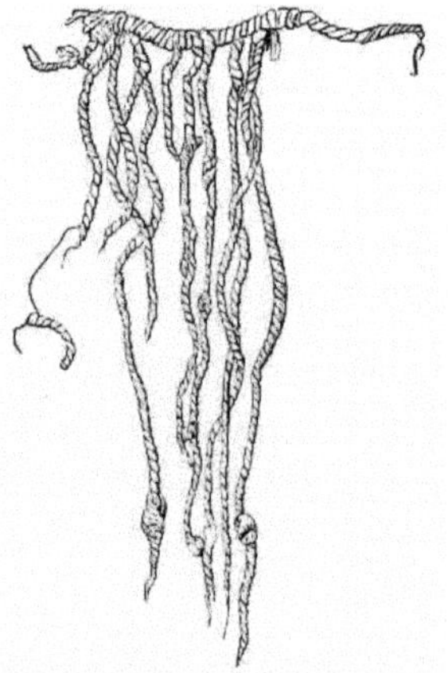

(a) The Mnemonic Stage.—This is well represented by "quipus" or knotted cords, and by wampums or shell-ornamented belts. The quipu (Fig. 7) has a long history, and is with us both in the rosary on which the Roman Catholic counts his prayers, in the knot which we tie in our handkerchief to help a weak memory, and in the sailor's log-line. Herodotus tells us that when Darius bade the Ionians remain to guard the floating bridge which spanned the Ister, he "tied sixty knots in a thong, saying: 'Men of Ionia ... do ye keep this thong and do as I shall say:—so soon as ye shall have seen me go forward against the Scythians, from that time begin and untie a knot on each day; and if within this time I am not here, and ye find that the days marked by the knots have passed by, then sail away to your own lands'" (iv. 98). And the same obviously handy device is of widespread use, reaching its more elaborate form among the ancient Peruvians, from whose language the term "quipu," meaning "knot," is borrowed. It consists of a main cord, to which are fastened at given distances thinner cords of different colours, each cord being knotted in divers ways for special purposes, and each colour having its own significance. Red strands stood for soldiers, yellow for gold, white for silver, green for corn, and so forth, while a single knot meant ten, two single knots meant twenty, double knots one hundred, and two double knots two hundred. Such simple devices served manifold purposes. Besides their convenience in reckoning, they were used for keeping the annals of the empire of the Incas; for transmitting orders to outlying provinces; for registering details of the army; and even for preserving records of the dead, with whom the quipu was buried, as in old Egypt the biography or titles of the deceased were set forth in hieroglyph and deposited in the tomb. Quoting from Von Tschudi's Peru, Dr. E. B. Tylor says that each town had its officer whose special function was to tie and interpret the quipus. They were called Quipucamayocuna, or knot-officers; but although they attained great facility in their work, they were seldom able to read a quipu without the aid of an oral commentary. When one came from a distant province, it was necessary to give notice with it whether it referred to census, tribute, war, and so forth. But by constant practice they so far perfected the system as to be able to register with their knots the most important events of the kingdom, and to set down its laws and ordinances. Although vain attempts to read the quipus have been made in the present day, Dr. Tylor adds that there are still Indians in Southern Peru "who are perfectly familiar with the contents of certain historical quipus preserved from ancient times; but they keep their knowledge a profound secret, especially from the white men." (Early History of Mankind, p. 160.) This knot-reckoning is in use among the Puna herdsmen of the Peruvian plateaux. On the first strand of the quipu they register the bulls, on the second the cows, these again they divide into milch-cows and those that are dry; the next strands register the calves, the next the sheep and so forth, while other strands record the produce; the different colours of the cords and the twisting of the knots giving the key to the several purposes. Akin to this is the practice among the Paloni Indians of California, concerning whom Dr. Hoffman reports that each year a certain number are chosen to visit the settlement at San Gabriel to sell native blankets. "Every Indian sending goods provided the salesman with two cords made of twisted hair or wool, on one of which was tied a knot for every real received, and on the other a knot for each blanket sold. When the sum reached ten reals, or one dollar, a double knot was made. Upon the return of the salesman, each person selected from the lot his own goods, by which he would at once perceive the amount due, and also the number of blankets for which the salesman was responsible." The natives of Ardrah, in West Africa, use small cords, each knot in which has a meaning; and among the Jebus, the objects knotted into strings tell their separate tale, cowrie shells placed face to face denoting friendship; an arrow, war; and so forth. Other tribes have devised message-sticks somewhat after the well-known native Australian type. More highly-developed knot-reckoning is found among the Mexican Zuni, and in more primitive form among some North American Indians; but, not tarrying to detail these, we cross the Pacific, noting, on our passage, that a generation ago the Hawaiian tax-gatherers kept accounts of the assessable property throughout the island on lines of cordage from four to five hundred fathoms long. Knots, loops, and tufts of different shape, size, and colour indicated the several districts, and the amount of tax to be paid by each inhabitant was defined by marks of the same character as those now specified, with such variety as to prevent confusion. The Shû-King, a sacred historical book of the Chinese, records the use of knotted cords prior to the invention of writing. The number and distances of the knots served as conventional mnemonics, and also as imperial records, until written characters replaced them. "Legend refers the tying of knots in strings to about 2800 B.C., when Fo-hi invented eight symbols, and at the same time pictorial representations of these knotted strings were taken to indicate the object thereby symbolised." These Morse-like symbols are:—

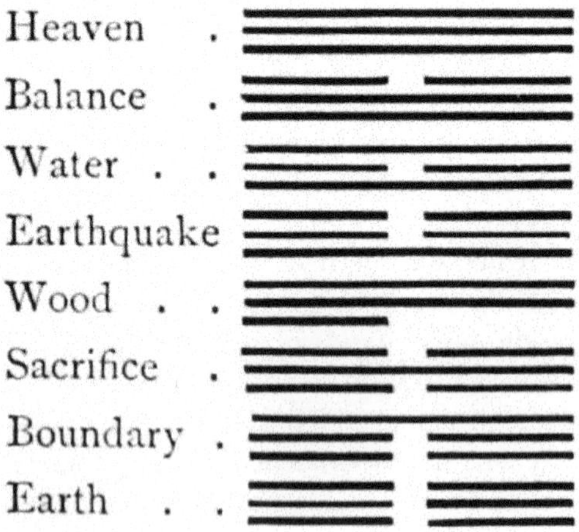

(C. Gardner, Journal Ethnological Society, 1870, vol. ii. p. 5)

Another Chinese legend says that "the most ancient forms were five hundred and forty characters, formed by a combination of knotted strings and the eight symbols, made in the form of birds' claws in various states of tension, and that all these five hundred and forty characters were suggested to the inventor by the marks (left by the claws) upon the sand." The use of looped or knotted cords is depicted in Egyptian hieroglyph, and among other tribes of the African continent the Jebus of to-day evidence the survival of this primitive memoria technica, while from Melanesia to Formosa the knotted cord, as in Australia and Africa the message-stick, render service as means of communication between man and his fellows. The nine incisions, with a longer cut across them to denote ten, is a mode of decimal reckoning and of record found alike among Red Indians and London bargees. The same purpose explains the custom, in force well within the present century, of our Exchequer in keeping certain accounts by means of notched tallies. The tally was a squared stick of well-seasoned hazel or willow, in one side of which notches of different breadth, indicating pounds, shillings, and pence, were cut to mark the amount of money lent by any person to the Government, the same amount being cut in Roman numerals, together with the lender's name and date of the loan, on the two opposite sides. The stick was then split down the middle, and one half handed to the lender, the other half being kept in the Exchequer. When the money fell due, the lender surrendered his half for comparison with its fellow, and the two being found to "tally," the loan was repaid. It was through the overheating of stoves in the burning of heaps of accumulated tally-sticks that the Houses of Parliament were destroyed in 1834. Fifty years ago in Scotland (and the like may happen in out-of-the-way hamlets to-day), the baker's boy took a "nick-stick" with his bread, and made a notch in the stick for every loaf he left on his rounds. So it was, Dr. Hoffman tells us, with the Pennsylvanian dairyman, who kept account of the milk which he sold by marking notches for pints and quarts on a stick. As these notches correspond to entries of transactions in our daybooks and ledgers, so the once widely-used Clog Almanack corresponded to our modern Whitaker. It consisted of a square-shaped "clog" or "block" of wood (sometimes of metal), and was designed chiefly to show when the Sundays and holidays fell, certain symbols or hieroglyphs being drawn against saint and other festal days—as, for example, an axe for Saint Paul, a true-lovers' knot for Saint Valentine, and a harp for Saint David. With this may be compared the hieroglyphic wheels named "record of the gods," formerly in use for recording time among the Indians of Virginia. "These wheels had sixty spokes, each for a year, as if to mark the ordinary age of man, and they were painted on skins kept by the priests. They marked on each spoke or division a hieroglyphic figure to show the memorable events of the year." (Tylor, p. 93.)

Wampum-belts are of much narrower geographical distribution than quipus. They consist of hand-made beads or perforated shells arranged in various more or less conventionalised patterns on bark filaments, hemp, or deerskin strips or sinews, the ends of the belts being selvedged by sinews or hempen fibres. The patterns are pictorial symbols recording events in the history of the tribe or treaties between tribes; the belts being also used to note land boundaries or personal property, sometimes even passing, in the old days, as shell-money in all parts of New England from one end of the coast to the other. As illustrating a common purpose for which the wampum record was used, Peter Clarke tells us, in his Origin and Traditional History of the Wyandotts (a tribe of the Huron-Iroquois stock), that "in the last decade of the eighteenth century, the king or head chief, Sut-staw-ra-tse, called a meeting at the house of Chief Adam Brown, who had charge of the archives, which consisted of wampum belts, parchments, &c., contained in a large trunk. One by one they were brought out and shown to the assembled chiefs and warriors. Chief Brown wrote on a piece of paper and tacked it to each wampum belt, designating the compact or treaty it represented, after it had been explained from memory by the chiefs appointed for that purpose. There sat before them the venerable king, in whose head were stored the hidden contents of each wampum belt, listening to the rehearsal, and occasionally correcting the speaker and putting him on the right track whenever he deviated." Clarke goes on to say that "when the majority of the people removed to the south-west, they demanded to have the belts, as these might be a safeguard to them. Some of these belts recorded treaties of alliance or of peace with other tribes which were now residing in that region, and it might be of great importance to the Wyandotts to be able to produce and refer to them. The justice of this claim was admitted, and they were allowed to have the greater part of their belts." And modern inquirers tell us that, in so far as the wampums still possess utility, it is as evidence of a subsisting treaty or a title-deed. Few examples, however, of the vast number of belts once in the possession of the North American tribes (and these almost exclusively confined to the Iroquois country) survive, since in the displacement of the red man by the white their value from the land-right point of view has disappeared. Four interesting specimens, known as the "Hale Series of Huron Wampum Belts," which were presented by Dr. Tylor to the Pitt-Rivers Museum at Oxford in 1897, form the subject of lengthy memoirs by the donor and the late Horatio Hale in the Journal of the Anthropological Institute (xxvi. 3, pp. 221-54). Of these only the barest summary is needful. The first and oldest example, dating from before the middle of the seventeenth century, is named the "Double Calumet Treaty Belt" (Figs. 8, 9). It is nine beads in width, and although imperfect, is still nearly four feet long. On a dark ground of the costly purple wampum there is the device of a council-hearth in what was probably the centre of the belt, flanked on one side by four and on the other side by three double calumets, i.e. double-headed peace-pipes, each possessing a bowl at both ends. Of course a pipe of this sort is of no use for smoking. It is a creation of the heraldic imagination, like the double-headed eagle of some modern European powers. This, first appearing on the arms of the German Emperor in the middle of the fourteenth century, may have been derived through contact with the East from Hittite bas-reliefs, as the cherub of our grave-stone cutters is derived through the Hebrews from the Assyrians, and the symbolic design of the Good Shepherd from the old type of Hermes, the ram-bearing god.

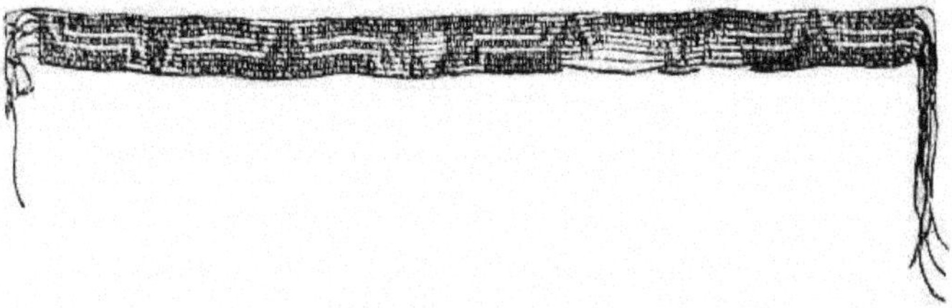

Fig. 8.—Double Calumet Wampum

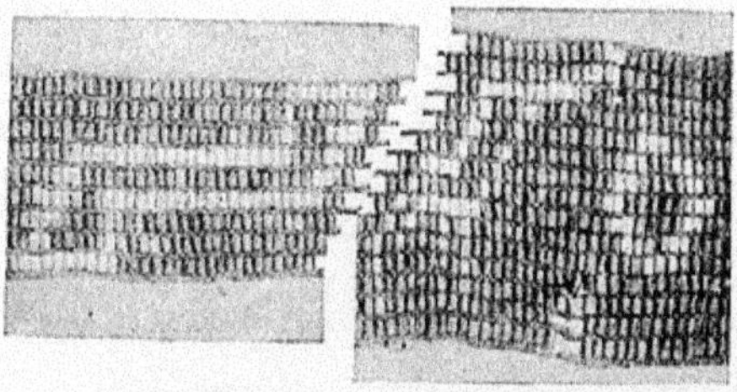

Fig. 9.—Double Calumet Council Hearth

Returning to the "double calumet," Mr. Hale was told by Mandorong, an Indian chief, that it was a peace-belt, representing an important treaty or alliance of ancient times. The second example is called Peace-Path Belt, which name indicates its purpose; the third, of which a good portion has probably vanished, is named the Jesuit Missionary Belt (Fig. 10), and is believed "to commemorate the acceptance by the Hurons of the Christian religion" as taught by the Jesuits.

Fig. 10.—Jesuit Missionary Wampum

Fig. 11.—Four Nations' Alliance Wampum

The figures are worked on fifteen rows of white beads on a dark ground, the oval or lozenge-shaped design near the centre representing a council. On each side of this are religious emblems—on one side the dove, on the other side the lamb—and beyond each are Greek crosses representing the Trinity. "The latest date which can be ascribed to this belt is the year 1648, the eve of the expulsion of the Hurons by the Iroquois." The fourth example (Fig. 11), called the "Four Nations' Alliance Belt," is sixty years younger, and, as denoted by the four squares forming the chief device, is a land-treaty made between the Wyandotts and three Algonquin tribes.

Fig. 11a.—Penn Wampum

This reference to records which mark a certain approach to the ideographic stage of writing would be incomplete if no account was given of the most celebrated wampum record in existence (Fig. 11a), the Penn Belt, preserved in the archives of the Historical Society of Pennsylvania. It derives its name from a well-authenticated tradition that it is the identical belt given, probably in 1701, to William Penn by the Iroquois "to confirm the friendly relations then permanently established between them." It is composed of eighteen strings of white wampum, thus evidencing its relation to an important transaction, and has in the centre two figures delineated in dark-coloured beads, one an Indian grasping the hand of a man who, as wearing a hat, is doubtless intended to represent a European. The oblique bands are the symbol of the federation of Iroquois known as the "Five Nations," and represent by synecdoche (or the putting of a part for the whole) the entire native Iroquois "long-house," as the communal dwelling is called. "The Iroquois league is spoken of in their Book of Rites as Kanastat-sikowa, the 'great framework.' It was this mighty structure, which, when the belt in question was given, overshadowed the greater part of North America, that was indicated by the rafters, shown as oblique bands." (Hale, J.A.I. xxvi. p. 244.)

(b) The Pictorial Stage.—The necessity of identifying personal as well as tribal property, especially in land and live stock, led to the employment of various characters more or less pictographic, which have their representatives in signaries used in ancient commerce and in manufacturers' trade marks. Professor Ernst of Caracas believes that he can recognise survivals of Indian picture-writing in the marks used for branding cattle; and among Mr. Arthur Evans's remarkable discoveries of pre-Mycenæan relics in Crete, the significance of which will be dealt with later on, are seal-stones engraved with signs which are not merely fanciful or ornamental, but designed to convey information about their owners. "For example, a boat with a crescent moon on either side of the mast may have been the signet of an ancient mariner who ventured on long voyages;" perchance a feat to be proud of, since even a one-moon voyage seems to have been too much for the average Homeric mariner (cf. Iliad, II. 292-4). "Another signet, with a gate and a pig on one of its faces, would be proper to a well-to-do swineherd." Other seals bearing the device of a fish may indicate a fisherman; of a harp, a musician, and so on. (The Mycenæan Age, p. 270: Tsountas and Manatt.) The painful operation of tattooing is known to have symbolic and religious, even more than decorative, significance, as marking the connection of the man with his clan-totem or individual totem. But it has also a utilitarian purpose, as among certain Red Indian tribes, who tattoo both sexes, so that in case of war the captured individuals may be identified and ransomed. Totemic and mythic animals are tattooed upon various parts of the body; in one case the design worn by a landowner among the Kavuya Indians of California was used as his property mark by being cut or painted upon boundary trees and posts, so that his title to his possessions was proved by the portable title-deed which he bore, reminding us of the leading incident in Rider Haggard's Mr. Meeson's Will. "In New Zealand the facial decorations of a dead man were reproduced upon the trees near his grave; while among the Yakuts and Bushmen the facial marks, or even totems, were furthermore employed as property marks, the Bushmen carving them upon growing squashes and melons." (Hoffman, p. 39.) The various Indian tribes appear to have made more frequent use of the totem name rather than of the personal name, perhaps because of the common barbaric notion that a man's name is an integral part of himself, through which, whether he be living or dead, mischief may be wrought by the sorcerer who knows the name—a notion the force of which would be lessened where the name is generic and shared in common. On the grave-posts of both Australian black fellows and North American Indians the totem symbol is reversed, as in our mediæval chronicles the leopards of English kings are reversed on the scutcheon drawn opposite the record of their death. With this we may connect the classic symbol of the inverted torch which the modern sculptor depicts on funereal monuments. In his great work on the History, Condition, and Prospects of the Indian Tribes, published over fifty years ago (a work, however, which needs checking from other authorities), Schoolcraft gives some illustrations of the red man's grave-posts, of which three are here reproduced.

Figs. 12, 13.—Indian Grave-posts

Fig. 14.—Tomb-board
of Indian Chief

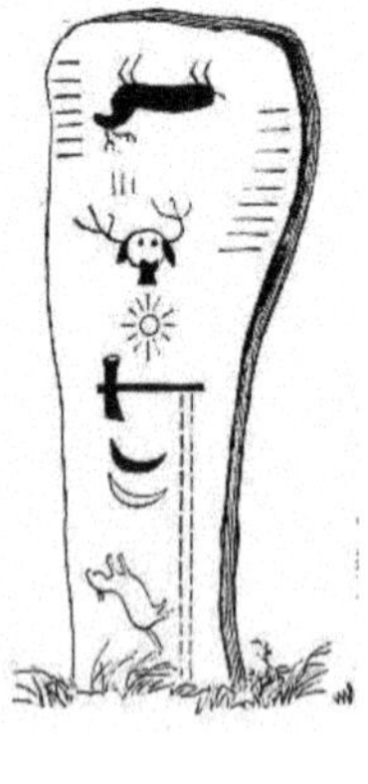

Fig. 12 shows the dead warrior's totem, a tortoise, and beside it a headless man, which is a common symbol of death among Indian tribes. Below the trunk are three marks of honour. The next and more elaborated figure (13) records the achievements of Shingabawassin, a celebrated chief of the St. Mary's band. His totem, the crane, is shown reversed. The three marks on the left of the totem represent important general treaties of peace to which he had been a party; the six strokes on the right probably indicate the number of big battles which he fought. The pipe appears to be a symbol of peace, and the hatchet a symbol of war. In like manner head-boards erected over a woman have the various articles used by her in life, as cutting and sewing instruments and weaving utensils, depicted upon them. The third example (14) represents the adjedatig or tomb-board of Wabojeeg, a celebrated war chief, who died on Lake Superior about 1793. His totem, the reindeer, is reversed, and his own name, which means the White Fisher, is not recorded. The seven strokes note the seven war parties whom he led; the three upright strokes as many wounds received in battle. The horned head tells of a desperate fight with a moose.

Fig. 15.—Hunter's Grave-post

Fig. 15 is a reduced copy (Hoffman) of the grave-board of an Innuit hunter. The vocation of the dead man is shown in the baidarka, or boat, in which he is depicted as rowing with a companion. The object beneath represents a rack for drying fish and skins. Next to this are figures of a fox and a land otter, and the network drawing at the bottom is a copy of the hunter's summer dwelling. These temporary structures denote the abode of a skin-hunter, those used by fishermen being dome-shaped. Hoffman adds that "this differentiation in the shape of roofs of habitations applies to their pictorial representation and not to their actual form." In close connection with these mortuary boards there is the ornamentation of door-posts which we find among British Columbian, Polynesian, and Maori tribes; also the carvings on canoes and other personal effects to mark ownership or to identify the property with the totem. But to pursue this would take us into the domain of savage art generally, reference to which is warranted here only in its mnemonic uses as keeping alive knowledge of events which would otherwise perish. Obviously, the examples given above can fulfil only a limited purpose, because only the initiated can know their meaning. As Dr. Tylor remarks, such mode of record "may be compared to the elliptical forms of expression current in all societies whose attention is given specially to some narrow subject of interest, and where, as all men's minds have the same framework set up in them, it is not necessary to go into an elaborate description of the whole state of things; but one or two details are enough to enable the hearer to understand the whole. Such expressions as 'new white at 48,' 'best selected at 92' ('futures fairly active' is a good example), though perfectly understood in the commercial circles where they are current, are as unintelligible to any one who is not familiar with the course of events in those circles, as an Indian record of a war-party would be to an ordinary Londoner." (Early History of Mankind, p. 86.) This applies with even greater force to the large group of symbolic mnemonics whose purpose is more restricted, whether it be as help to the singer in his verses, to the medicine-man in his incantation, to the hunter in his quest, or, as among ourselves, to the tramp on his rounds. The subjoined copy of a cadger's map (Fig. 16), given in Hotten's Slang Dictionary (1869), is an addition to the number of survivals which are found in so-called civilised communities, and has fit place among the examples of pictorial mnemonics in matters of 1, love; 2, sorcery; 3, the chase; 4, war; and 5, politics which follow it.

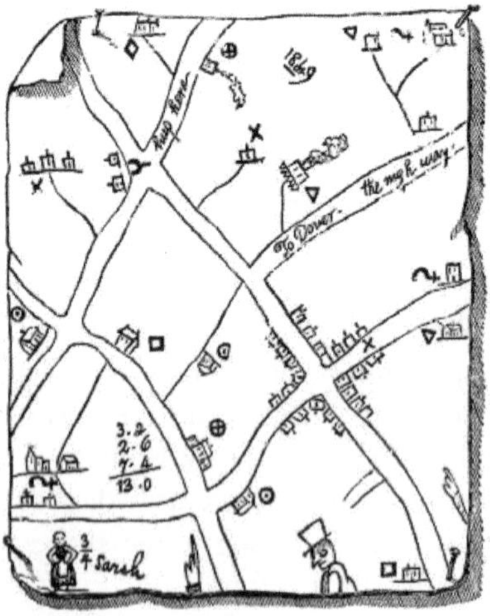

Fig. 16.—A Cadger's Map of a Begging District

Explanation of the Hieroglyphics

× No Good; too poor, and know too much.
⌒+ Stop. If you have what they want, they'll buy. They are pretty *fly* (knowing).
⊃– Go this Way; better than the other road. Nothing that way.
◇ Bone (good). Safe for a "cold tatur." *Cheese your patter* (don't talk much).
▽ Cooper'd (spoilt) by too many calling there.
▭ Gammy (unfavourable); likely to have you taken up. Mind the dog.
⊙ Flummuxed (dangerous); sure of a month in *quod* (prison).
⊕ Religious, but tidy on the whole.

1. Love.—Fig. 17 is a reduced copy of a love-letter, drawn upon birch bark (a material used elsewhere, as among the Yukaghirs of Siberia), which an Ojibwa girl sent to her sweetheart at White Earth, Minnesota. She was of the "Bear" totem, he of the "Mud Puppy" totem; hence the picture of these animals as representing the addresser and the addressee. The two lines from their respective camps meet and are continued to a point between two lakes, another trail branching off towards two tents. Here three girls, Catholic converts, as denoted by the three crosses, are encamped, the left-hand tent having an opening from which an arm protrudes with beckoning gesture. The arm is that of the writer of the letter, who is making the Indian sign of welcome to her lover. "This is done by holding the palm of the hand down and forward, and drawing the extended index finger towards the place occupied by the speaker, thus indicating the path upon the ground to be followed by the person called."

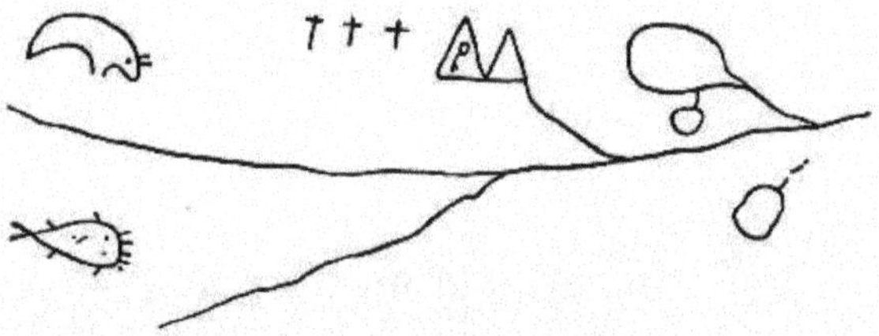

Fig. 17.—Ojibwa Love-letter

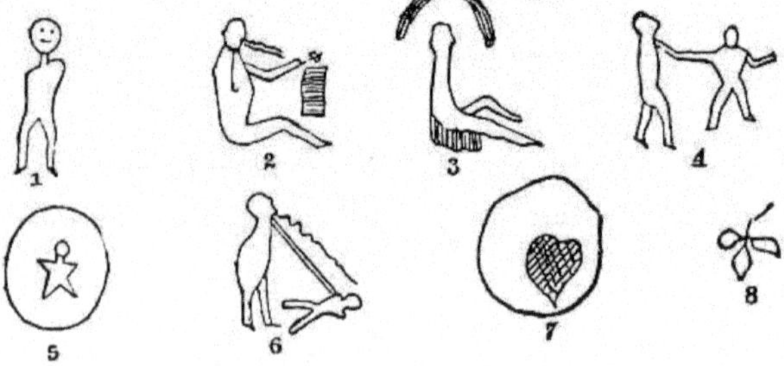

Fig. 18.—Love-song

Fig. 18 is the record of a love-song. 1, represents the lover; 2, he is singing and beating a magic drum; in 3, he surrounds himself with a secret lodge, denoting the effects of his necromancy; in 4, he and his mistress are joined by a single arm to show that they are as one; in 5, she is on an island; in 6, she sleeps, and as he sings, his magical power reaches her heart; and in 7, the heart itself is shown. To each of these figures a verse of the song corresponds.

1. It is my painting that makes me a god. 2. Hear the sounds of my voice, of my song; it is my voice. 3. I cover myself in sitting down by her. 4. I can make her blush, because I hear all she says of me. 5. Were she on a distant island I could make her swim over, 6. Though she were far off, even on the other hemisphere. 7. I speak to your heart.

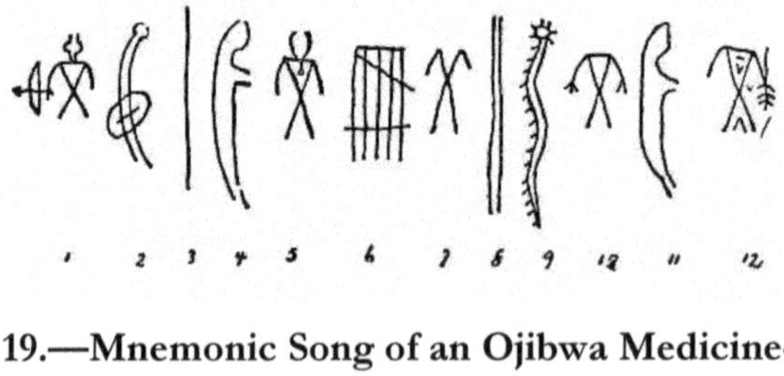

Fig. 19.—Mnemonic Song of an Ojibwa Medicine-man.

2. Sorcery.—Fig. 19 is the song of an Ojibwa medicine-man incised upon birch bark. These conjurers, who correspond to the Siberian shamans, affect the usual mystery of the priestly craft all the world over, and affirm, like those who know better, that their thaumaturgic powers are the direct gift of the god. Him they name Manabozho—probably some ancestral deity, since he is the great uncle of the anish'inabēg or "first people." In 1, Manabozho holds his bow and arrow; 2, represents the medicine-man's drum and drumsticks used in chanting and in initiation ceremonies; 3, a bar

or rest observed while chanting the incantation; 4, the medicine-bag, made of an otter skin, in which is preserved the white cowrie shell as the sacred emblem of the cult; 5, the medicine-man himself, horned to show his superior power; 6, a funnel-like object, known as a "jugglery," used in legerdemain and other hocus pocus; 7, a woman, signifying the admission of her sex to "the society of the grand medicine"; 8, a bar or rest, as at 3; 9, the sacred snake-skin medicine bag, which has magic power; 10, another woman; 11, another otter-skin "bag o' tricks," showing that women members are allowed to use it; 12, a female figure, holding a branch of some sacred plant used in the exorcism of the demon of disease. In any reference to savage therapeutics it cannot be too often insisted upon that diseases are never ascribed to natural causes. "The Indians believed that diseases were caused by unseen evil beings and by witchcraft, and every cough, every toothache, every headache, every fever, every boil, and every wound, in fact all their ailments, were attributed to such a cause. Their so-called medical practice was a horrible system of sorcery, and to such superstition human life was sacrificed on an enormous scale.... In fact, a natural death in a savage tent is a comparatively rare phenomenon; but death by sorcery, medicine, and blood-feud arising from a belief in witchcraft is exceedingly common." (Professor Powell's Indian Linguistic Families of America North of Mexico, p. 39.)

Fig. 20.—Wâbeno destroying an Enemy

Fig. 20 records the destruction of an enemy by an Ojibwa wâbeno or bad medicine-man. The box-like objects represent the four degrees of the cult society to which the wâbeno belonged, the number of posts indicating the series. The figure next to these is that of the assistant to the wâbeno, who is shown with a waving line extending from his mouth to the oval-like object intended to represent a lake upon an island in which the victim lives. He is shown prostrate beneath the wâbeno with a spot upon his breast, the small oblong figure between the two being the sacred drum. (See 2 in the foregoing illustration.) The meaning of the pictograph is that the wâbeno was employed to work black magic on the man. He took a piece of birch bark and cut upon it the effigy of the victim, then, after beating the drum to the chanting of incantations, he pierced the breast of the effigy, applying red paint to the puncture. This, under the principle of "sympathetic magic," was believed to bring about the death of the victim, whom, through his living on the island, the wâbeno could not reach.

Fig. 21.—Etching on Innuit Drill-bow

White magic, in which the beneficent powers are at work, is illustrated by the Innuit pictograph on an ivory drill-bow (Fig. 21), on the right of which are two huts, nearest to which stands the medicine-man who has been called in to exorcise the disease from a couple of sufferers. He is catching hold of the animal by whose help the disease-demon is expelled, or to whom, mayhap, as a sort of scapegoat, the disease is transferred. In the second exorcism, the medicine-man is grasping the patient by the arm, while he chants the formulæ wherewith to cast out the demon. The figure on the left is making a gesture of surprise at his relief, while beyond him are two demons struggling to escape beyond the power of the medicine man.

Fig. 22.—Ojibwa Hunting Record

3. The Chase.—Fig. 22 records a hunting expedition. The two lines represent a wave-tossed river, on which floats a bark canoe, guided by the owner. In the bow a piece of birch bark shields a fire of pine knots to light up the course taken by the steersman. By this means the game, as it comes to the water to drink, can be seen from the shaded part of the canoe, in front of which two deer are shown. Next to these is a circle representing a lake, from which peep the head and horns of a third deer. To the right of the lake a doe appears, and beyond her the two wigwams of the hunter. The four animals may represent the quarry secured.

Fig. 23.—Hidatsa Pictograph on a Buffalo Shoulder-blade

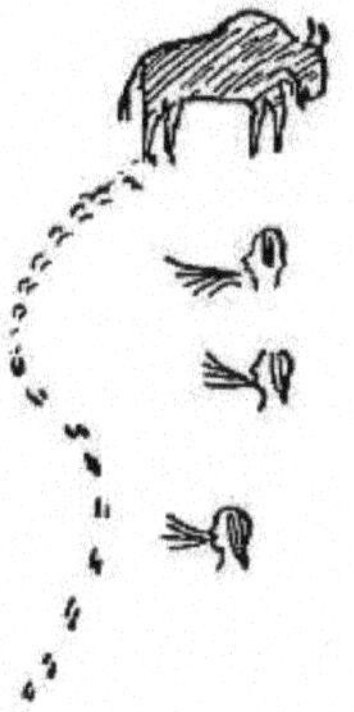

Fig. 23, drawn on a buffalo shoulder-blade by a Hidatsa Indian, tells his efforts to track companions who had gone buffalo-hunting. The trail of the animal and the pursuers is shown in the dotted lines. Of the three heads the lowest is that of the seeker, who is depicted shouting after his missing friends; then he is shown advancing and still shouting, till his call is returned from the spot where the hunters have camped.

Fig. 24.—Alaskan Hunting Record

Fig. 25.—Record of Starving Hunter

Fig. 24, incised on an ivory drill-bow, is a pictograph of an Alaskan sea-lion hunt. In 1, the speaker points with his left hand in the direction to be taken, and, 2, holds a paddle to show that a voyage is intended. In 3, the right hand to the side of the head denotes sleep, while the left hand with one finger elevated means one night. The circle with two dots in the middle, 4, signifies an island with huts; 5 is the same as 1; 6 is another island; 7 is the same as 3, but with two fingers elevated to indicate two nights. In 8 the speaker with his harpoon makes the sign of a sea-lion with his left hand, which he thrusts outward and downward in a slight curve to represent the animal swimming; 9, 10, a sea-lion shot at with bow and arrow; 11, two men in a boat, the paddles pushed downwards; and 12, the speaker's hut. The native account, as translated, reads thus: "I there go that island, one sleep there; then I go another that island, there two sleeps; I catch one sea-lion, then return mine." (Colonel Mallery, quo. Hoffman, Transactions of the Anthropological Society, Washington, vol. ii. p. 134, 1883.) "Hunters who have been unfortunate, and are starving, scratch or draw upon a piece of wood characters like those in Fig. 25, and place the lower end of the stick in the ground on the trail where it is most likely to be discovered," the stick being inclined towards the hunter's dwelling. The horizontal line 1, denotes a canoe, 2, the gesture of the man with both arms extended, signifies "nothing," while the uplifting of the right hand to the mouth, 3, means "food" or "to eat," and the left hand outstretched points to 4, the hut of the famished man. Here we are actually within the ideographic stage, and, as will be shown in due course, handling material identical in character with that found in Egypt and other nations of antiquity. But, as already remarked, and as will be evidenced in abundance throughout these pages, there are no well-marked divisions between the stages of development.

A varied interest attaches to Fig. 26, which depicts some general features of Alaskan life on a piece of walrus tusk. In 1, a native is resting against his house, and on his right stands a pole surmounted by a bird, apparently a totem-post. 2. A reindeer. 3. One man shooting at another with an arrow. 4. An expedition in a dog-sledge, and, 5, in a boat with sail and paddle. 6. A dog-sledge, with the sun above; perhaps indicating the coming of summer. 7. A sacred lodge. The four figures at each outer corner represent young men armed with bows and arrows to keep off the uninitiated from the forbidden precincts. The members of the occult society are dancing round a fire in the centre of the lodge. 8. A pine tree up which a porcupine is climbing. 9. Another pine tree, from which a woodpecker is extracting larvæ. 10. A bear. 11, 12. Men driving fish into, 13, the net, above them being a captured whale, with harpoon and line attached.

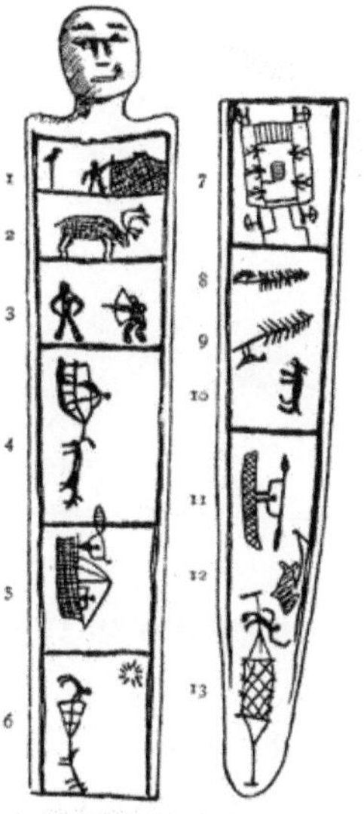

Fig. 26.—Alaskan Hunting Life

4. War.—Schoolcraft, who has been already drawn upon for an example (page 53), records the finding of the bark letter copied in Fig. 27. It was fastened to the top of a pole so as to attract the notice of other Indians who might happen to be passing. Beginning on the right of the middle row we have 1, the officer in command, sword in hand; 2, his secretary, and 3, the geologist of the party, indicated by his hammer. Then follow 4, 5, two attachés; 6, the interpreter; and 7, 8, two Chippewa guides. In the top row is 9, 10, a group of seven soldiers, armed with muskets. A prairie hen and tortoise, 11, 12, represent the animals secured for food.

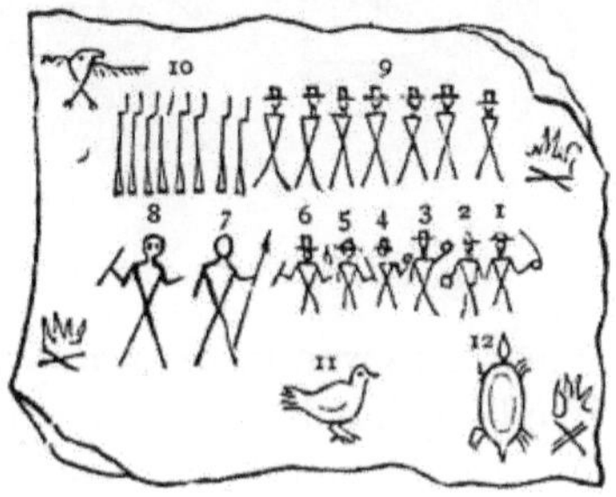

Fig. 27.—Indian Expedition

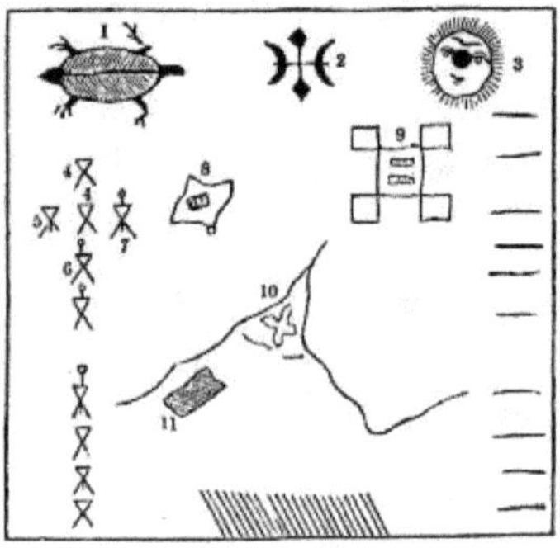

Fig. 28.—Biography of Indian Chief

Fig. 28 gives the biography of Wingemund, a noted Delaware chief. To the left is 1, the tortoise totem of the tribe; then 2, the chief-totem; and 3, the sun, beneath which are ten strokes representing the ten expeditions in which Wingemund took part. On the opposite side are indicated, 4, 5, 6, 7, the prisoners of both sexes taken, and also the killed, these last being drawn as headless. In the centre are the several positions attacked, 8, 9, 10, 11; and the slanting strokes at the bottom denote the number of Wingemund's followers.

Fig. 29.—War-song

Fig. 29 is a war-song. Wings are given to the warrior, 1, to show that he is swift-footed; in 2 he stands under the morning star, and in 3 under the centre of heaven, with his war-club and rattle; in 4, the eagles of carnage are flying round the sky; in 5, the warrior lies slain on the battlefield; while in 6 he appears as a spirit in the sky. The words of the song are as follows:—

1. I wish to have the body of the swiftest bird. 2. Every day I look at you; the half of the day I sing my song. 3. I throw away my body. 4. The birds

take a flight in the air. 5. Full happy am I to be numbered with the slain. 6. The spirits on high repeat my name.

5. Political and Social.—The frontispiece is a copy of a petition sent by a group of Indian tribes to the United States Congress for fishing rights in certain small lakes near Lake Superior. The leading clan is represented by Oshcabawis, whose totem is 1, the crane; then follow 2, Waimitligzhig; 3, Ogemagee; and 4, a third, all of the marten totem; 5, Little Elk, of the bear totem; 6, belongs to the manfish totem; 7, to the catfish totem.

From the eye and heart of each of the animals runs a line connecting them with the eye and heart of the crane to show that they are all of one mind, and the eye of the crane has also a line connecting it with the lakes on which the tribes want to fish, while another line runs towards Congress.

Fig. 30 is a copy of a letter found above St. Anthony's Falls in 1820. "It consisted of white birch bark, and the figures had been carefully drawn. 1, Denotes the flag of the Union; 2, the cantonment then recently established at Cold Spring, on the western side of the cliffs; 4 is the symbol of Colonel Leavenworth, the commanding officer, under whose authority a mission of peace had been sent into the Chippewa country; 11 is the symbol of Chakope, the leading Sioux chief, under whose orders the party moved; 8 is the second chief, named Wabedatunka, or, 10, the Black Dog, who has fourteen lodges, 7 is a chief also subordinate to Chakope, with thirteen lodges, and 9 is a bale of goods devoted by the Government to the objects of the peace. The name of 6, whose wigwam is 5, with thirteen subordinate lodges, was not given."

The letter was written to make known the fact that Chakope and his followers, accompanied or supported by the American officer, had come to the spot to make peace with the Chippewa hunters. "The Chippewa chief, Babesacundabee, who found the letter, read off its meaning without doubt or hesitation." (Schoolcraft, vol. i. p. 352.)

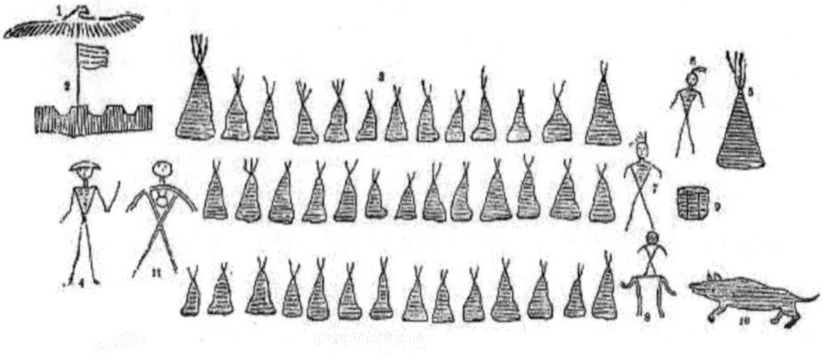

Fig. 30.—Letter offering Treaty of Peace

Fig. 31 represents the census roll of an Indian band at Mille Lac, in the territory of Minnesota, sent in to the United States agent by Nagonabe, a Chippewa Indian, during the annuity payments in 1849.

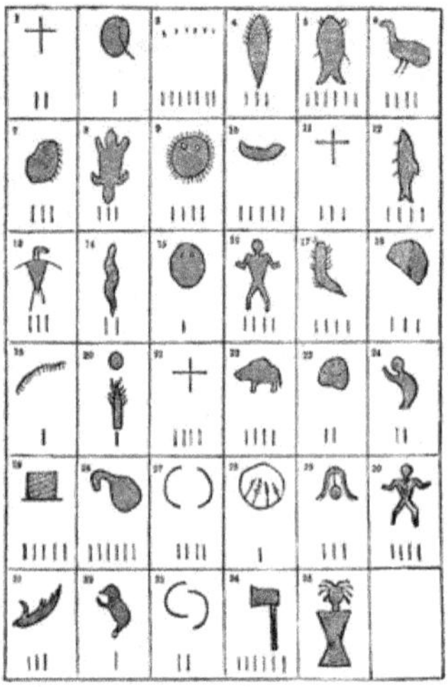

Fig. 31.—Census Roll of an Indian Band

As the Indians were all of the same totem, Nagonabe "designated each family by a sign denoting the common name of the chief. Thus 5 denotes a catfish, and the six strokes indicate that the Catfish's family consisted of six individuals; 8 is a beaver skin; 9, a sun; 13, an eagle; 14, a snake; 22, a buffalo; 34, an axe; 35, the medicine-man, and so on." (Lubbock, Origin of Civilisation, p. 47.)

Fig. 32.—Record of Departure (Innuit)

Fig. 32 supplies a striking example of the cumbersomeness of the pictograph as contrasted with the sound-symbol. It is a copy of a record which an Innuit placed over the door of his dwelling to notify to his friends that he had gone on a journey. The persons thus notified are indicated in 1, 3, 5, 7; 2 is the speaker, who denotes the direction in which he is leaving by his extended left hand; 4 is the gesture sign for "many," and 6 for sleep, the upraising of the left hand showing that he will be some distance away; 8, his intended return is denoted by the right hand being pointed homeward, while the left arm is bent to denote return.

(c) The Ideographic Stage.—As the characters pass from the pictorial to the emblematic or the symbolic, their meaning, obviously, becomes more obscure, save to the initiated. "They do not," as Colonel Mallery remarks, "depict, but suggest objects; do not speak directly through the eye to the intelligence, but presuppose in the mind knowledge of an event or fact which the sign recalls. The symbols of the ark, dove, olive-branch, and rainbow would be wholly meaningless to people unfamiliar with the Mosaic or some similar cosmology, as would be the cross and the crescent to those ignorant of history." And even in pictography, as the same excellent authority observes, "it is very difficult, if not impossible, to distinguish between historical and traditional accounts obtained from Indians. The winter counts (i.e. the reckoning of time by winters, and the applying of names instead of numbers to them, as, e.g., 'catching-wild-horses winter,' the device for which was a lasso), while having their chief value as calendars, contain some material that is absolute and verifiable tribal history." The difficulties of interpretation, as the examples given evidence, are in the larger number being "merely mnemonic records, and treated in connection with material objects formerly, and perhaps still, used mnemonically." (Mallery, "On the Pictographs of the North American Indians," Fourth Annual Report of the Bureau of Ethnology, 1886.)

The signs of advance from the pictorial to the ideographic stage which are to be noted among the Red Indians, are more sharply marked in the hieroglyphs and phonetic characters on the stone monuments and manuscripts found among the relics of the vanished peoples of Mexico and Yucatan.

A number of fatuous theories about the connection of Central American culture with that of the Old World have been broached, from the time when Lord Kingsborough published his lavishly-illustrated book to prove that the ancient Mexicans were the descendants of the lost Ten Tribes of Israel to the present day, when Dr. Augustus Le Plongeon brings us his "proofs" that Yucatan was the primitive home of Adam, and avers that he has discovered not only the grave of Abel, but disinterred his heart therefrom, and found the knife wherewith Cain slew him! (Queen Moo and the Egyptian Sphinx, p. 138.) Now, among the certainties which modern research has reached is that of the independent origin and development of civilisation in the New World. Man himself, whether or not descended from a single pair, had his origin in one region, probably the Indo-Malaysian, since there we find his nearest congeners, the anthropoid apes, while the pliocene beds of Java have recently yielded a remarkable corroboration of the theory in the fossil bones which bring man near to the common stem whence the highest animals have diverged. At a period when the general temperature of the globe was milder than now, the ancestors of the existing four leading groups—the Ethiopic, Mongolic, American, and Caucasic—spread themselves over the several zones of the habitable world, the American group migrating from Asia and Europe across the then existing land-connection between those continents and the New World, where those various stages of development which are still to be witnessed from the Arctic regions to Cape Horn were reached. Of these the Mexican plateau affords interesting and valuable material in the chipped flint implements evidencing a Stone Age, and in the marvellous buildings which vie both in their cyclopean dimensions and ornamented features with the palaces, tombs, and temples of Egypt and Assyria, testifying to the relatively high culture of the races that raised them. These peoples, usually grouped together as the ancient Mexicans, are known as Mayas and Aztecs. The duration of the empire or confederation of the Mayas is unknown, but about two hundred years before the Spanish conquest of America they appear to have been invaded and subdued by the Aztecs, whose rule extended from the Atlantic to the Pacific in the countries now forming Mexico and portions of the United States. The remains of the two races are both imperfect and entangled, so that any coherent story is not to be extracted from them. But the evidence points to the Mayas as the intellectually superior race; the Aztecs, who still form the bulk of the population of South Mexico, borrowing largely from them, especially in the matter of the gods. "If written language be a test of intelligence, the Mayas were ahead not only of the Mexican people, but also of the Peruvians. The latter are believed to have made no nearer advance towards writing than the tying of tally-knots on strings, and the Mexicans, while they had invented paper, wrote down their ideas, save in the cases of a few phonetic signs, as children would, by means of pictures; but the Mayas, like the Egyptians, had proceeded beyond pictures to hieroglyphs, where symbols, more or less arbitrary, stand for words or syllables, and the mind prepares itself to invent an alphabet." (Mercer's Hill Caves of Yucatan, p. 73.) Some of the more remarkable hieroglyphic-bearing monuments of the Mayas have been found in the palace of Palenque, the Spanish name of the old Yucatan capital. They are on stucco slabs above figures some of which show curious correspondence to Egyptian statues, wearing the pleasant but immobile expression of the latter, and decorated with a similar headdress, while in one case (Fig. 33), a cartouche enclosing an inscription is carved on the plinth. The concluding panels of one of the codices form what may be called the Mexican Book of the Dead. It enforces the scheme of duty which precedes by vividly depicting the trial and judgment of the soul after death, and detailing the perils of the journey on the way to Mictlan (Payne, ii. 407).

Fig. 33.—Statue from Palenque

Time and fanaticism have made sad havoc with the manuscripts, and no satisfactory key to their decipherment has been found, only a few words here and there being interpreted. They were executed in bright and varied colours, with a feather pencil, on prepared skins, paper, or rolls of cotton or aloe-fibre cloth, and the pictographic system thus created was applied to the purposes of ordinary life, and served as a species of writing. Matters of only passing importance were recorded on fibrous paper made from the leaves of the maguey plant; "records intended to be permanently kept were painted on the prepared skins of animals, those of the deer and bear being more commonly used. These paintings or 'pinturos' are usually executed on both sides of the skin, which was oblong in shape and often of great length, having the ends protected by boards." (Payne's History of the New World called America, vol. ii. p. 404.) These boards are called analtees, a word which may be translated annals. The earlier hieroglyphic characters were executed by priests, who were required to be old men, widowers, and under vows of chastity and seclusion. Such writing was known only to the initiated.

Tradition says that the Aztecs destroyed many of the Maya picture records because they recalled the grandeur of the conquered people. But the Spaniards in their turn destroyed much more. Zumárraga, Bishop of Mexico, and Landa, Bishop of Yucatan, made such bonfires of carvings, statues, paintings on wood, and of priceless picture and hieroglyph writings on native paper and deerskin, that only about half-a-dozen fragments of the Yucatan books have ever been found since. Bishop Landa, probably from knowledge obtained from Maya priests, attempted the framing of a key of interpretation, his aim being the translation of certain religious and devotional writings for the use of converts. In this he indicates a certain number of alphabetic characters, but the key did not work, and Dr. Isaac Taylor draws the conclusion that "the systems of picture-writing which were invented and developed by the tribes of Central America are so obscure, and so little is really known about their history, that they must be regarded rather as literary curiosities than as affording suitable materials for enabling us to arrive at any general conclusions as to the nature of the early stages of the development of the graphic art." (Hist. Alph., i. 24.) Notwithstanding this somewhat sweeping verdict, the Maya-Aztec scripts have value, if only for purposes of comparison. There is preserved in the museum at Mexico a whole series of pictographs exhibiting incidents as varied as the migrations of tribes, the annals of the people, sacrifices to the gods, and the education of children, the tasks set them, the punishments inflicted on them, and the food given them. To the hieroglyph there succeeds the gradually conventionalised sign, of which examples from Red Indian scripts have been given:—the arrow, to denote an enemy; several arrows, several enemies; the direction of the arrow's point, the direction taken by the enemy; a piece of maize cake protruding from the mouth, to denote eating; the symbol for water between the lips, to signify drinking; horizontal lines, with arrow-headed characters on them, to denote the hoed or cultivated ground, some of these ideographs being coloured to correspond with the thing suggested; and, as an example of the more abstruse, the extended arms, probably to denote negation,—all marking the advance to phonetic syllabic writing. The names of persons and places are sometimes indicated by symbolic figures; e.g. Chapultepec, or "grasshopper hill," is represented by a hill and a grasshopper; Tzompanco, "the place of skulls," by a skull on a bar between two posts, as enemies' skulls used to be set up; and Macuilxochitl, the "five flowers," by five dots and a flower. Sometimes we find the species of pun known as the rebus adopted. A picture is made to stand for the sound of the word, as e.g. among ourselves in guessing games, when a whisk broom and a key stand for "whiskey," or in the series of pictures of an eye, a saw, a boy, a swallow, a goose, and a berry, which stand for the sentence, "I saw a boy swallow a goose-berry." In Abbot Islip's Chapel in Westminster Abbey his name is rebused as an eye and the slip of a tree with the hand apparently of a slipping man hanging to it. In Bishop Oldham's chantry in Exeter Cathedral his name is represented by an owl (Owle-dom, the old spelling of the name); and in St. Saviour's Church the name of Prior Burton is sculptured as a cask with a thistle on it, "burr-tun."

Fig. 34.—Itzcoatl

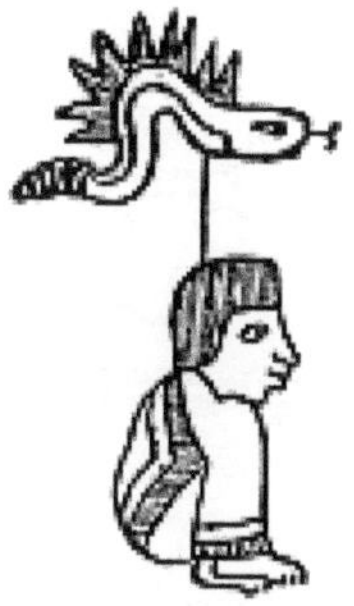

(d) The Phonetic Stage.—The ancient Mexican script supplies examples of the change from the pictographic to the phonetic stage. The name of one of the kings was Itzcoatl, or "Knife-Snake." In the manuscript known as the Le Tellier Codex this king's name (Fig. 34) is represented by a serpent (coatl) with stone knives (itzli) upon its back. This is mere picture-writing, but in the Vergara Codex we find the rebus form (Fig. 35). "The first syllable, itz, is represented by a weapon armed with blades of obsidian, itz (tli), but the rest of the word, coatl, though it means snake, is written, not by a picture of a snake, but by an earthen pot, co (mitl), and above it the sign of water, a (tl). Here we have real phonetic writing, for the name is not to be read, according to sense, 'knife-kettle-water,' but only according to the sound of the Aztec words, Itz-co-atl." Dr. Tylor adds that there is no sufficient reason to make us doubt that this purely phonetic writing was of native Mexican origin, and that after the Spanish Conquest it was turned to account in a new and curious way. The Spanish missionaries, when embarrassed by the difficulty of getting the converts to remember their Ave Marias and Paternosters, seeing that the words were, of course, mere nonsense to them, were helped out by the Indians themselves, who substituted Aztec words as near in sound as might be to the Latin, and wrote down the pictured equivalents for these words, which enabled them to remember the required formulas. Torquemada and Las Casas have recorded two instances of this device.

Fig. 35.—Rebus
of Itzcoatl

Pater noster was written by a flag (pantli) and a prickly pear (nochtli), while the sign of water, a (tl) combined with that of aloe, me (tl), made a compound word, ametl, which would mean "water-aloe," but in sound made a very tolerable substitute for Amen. M. Aubin found the beginning of a Paternoster of this kind in the metropolitan library of Mexico (Fig. 36), made with a flag, pan (tli), a stone, te (tl), a prickly pear, noch (tli), and again a stone, te (tl), which would read Pa-te-noch-te, or perhaps Pa-tetl-noch-tetl. After the conquest, when the Spaniards were hard at work introducing their own religion and civilisation among the conquered Mexicans, they found it convenient to allow the old picture-writing still to be used, even in legal documents. It disappeared in time, of course, being superseded in the long run by the alphabet, and it is to this transition period that we owe many, perhaps most, of the picture documents still preserved. "One of the picture-writings in the museum at Mexico is very probably the same that was sent up to Vera Cruz, to Montezuma, with figures of newly-arrived white men, their ships and horses, and their cannon with fire and smoke issuing from their mouths." (Tylor, Anahuac, p. 232.) In the general history of the development of writing, the Mexican script therefore supplies us only with an example of approximation to the phonetic system, its advance to the final alphabetic stage being probably arrested by the subjugation of the Mayas to an intellectually inferior conqueror, who, borrowing much, and contributing nothing of advantage, himself yielded to the superior force of Spain.

Fig. 36.—Paternoster Rebus

CHAPTER IV
THE CHINESE, JAPANESE, AND COREAN SCRIPTS

China, whose inertia is being aroused by foreign "pin-pricks," is the land of arrested developments, and consequently its writing has remained for probably two thousand years at a rudimentary stage, furnishing an interesting object-lesson on the early processes of advance, after the disuse of knotted cords (see p. 43), from the Ku-wăn, or "ancient pictures," to the Ling-shing, or "pictures and sounds." The language has never got beyond the monosyllabic stage; it has no terminations to denote number, case, tense, mood, or person, the same word without change of form being used as a noun, verb, or other "part of speech," so that a sentence can be construed only by the place of the several words composing it. As Dr. Marshman tersely puts it, "the whole of Chinese grammar depends upon position." For example, while the root-meaning of ta is "being great," it may, as a noun, mean "greatness"; as an adjective, "great"; as a verb, "to be great," or "to make great"; and as an adverb, "greatly." And, moreover, not only position, but also tone and gesture, contribute to the interpretation of the spoken language.

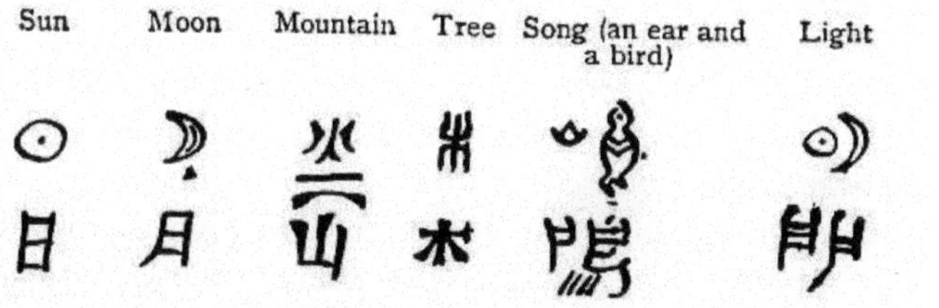

Fig. 37.—Chinese Picture-writing and Later Uncial

The characters fall into six wen or classes:—1, pictorial, giving a picture of the thing itself; 2, indicative, i.e. designed by their form and the relation of their parts to suggest the idea in the mind of their inventor; 3, composite, i.e. made up of two characters, the meanings of which blend in the meanings of the compounds; 4, inverted, or, as the term implies, topsy-turvy; 5, borrowed, i.e. having another meaning attached to them; 6, phonetic, i.e. one part indicating the sense and another part the sound. In Chinese phrase the ideogram is the "mother of meaning" and the phonogram the "mother of sound." The materials used largely determine the form which writing takes, and in the modern or cursive characters which are shown underneath the primitive forms we see the result of use of the rabbit's-hair pencil of the Chinese scribe. Respecting the first class, it suffices to say little, because it explains itself (Fig. 37). The sun was drawn as a circle, the moon as a crescent, a mountain was indicated by three peaks, rain by drops under an arch, and so forth. But, as has been sufficiently shown, such devices carry us a very little way; there is no literature possible under a mere graphic system. The third, or composite class, is the most interesting as supplying the key to the common idea of the character represented. Sometimes the characters indicate a dry humour. A "wife" is denoted by the signs for "female" and "broom," a sort of metonymy for a woman's household work; for a male child the signs "field" and "strength" are used, because he will till the soil. The Chinese, it will be remembered, are a purely agricultural people, and the compound for "profit" is "grain" and "a knife." The characters for "mountain" and "man" signify "hermit"; an "eye" and "water" mean "tears"; and the verb "to listen" is indicated by an ear between two doors. The signs for the noonday sun are the "sun" and "to reign"; "light" as an abstract quality is represented by figures of the sun and moon placed side by side; a "man" and "two" stand for mankind; a couple of women stand for "strife," three for "intrigue," while a "woman under two trees" means "desire" or "covetousness." But the inadequacy of these and the other symbols to supply characters for the demands of a language in which the same sound has to stand for a multitude of ideas gave rise to the phonetic group, whose development from picture-writing more or less ideographic took place many centuries b.c. The primary symbols or combinations of vowels and consonants number about four hundred and fifty. The variations in tone in pronouncing these sounds increase the total of monosyllabic words to be understood by the ear to something over twelve hundred. But the Chinese dictionaries contain above forty thousand words, and it is the symbols for each of these which are provided by the phonetic symbols. These were compound signs, the first character, as shown above, being a phonogram or sound-word, and the second character a determinative, i.e. ideogram or sense-word. They are, as Professor Whitney says, "rather an auxiliary language than a reduction of speech to writing." The sign for "man" has nearly six hundred combinations, all denoting something relating to man; that for "tree" has about nine hundred, to indicate various kinds of trees and wood, things made of wood, and so forth; while, to borrow a concrete example, pe, which means "white," has, with a "tree" prefixed, the meaning of "cypress"; with the sign for "man" it means "elder brother"; with the sign for "manes" it means the vital principle that survives death; and so forth. Chow is the Chinese word for "ship," so a picture of a ship stands for the sound chow. But the word chow means several other things, and the determinative or "key" sign indicates these. "Thus the ship joined with the sign of water stands for chow, 'ripple'; with that of speech for chow, 'loquacity'; with that of fire for chow, 'flickering of flame,' and so on for 'waggon-pole,' 'fluff,' and several other things which have little in common but the name of chow" (Tylor, p. 102). Although, theoretically, the Chinaman has to make an enormous number of characters before he can write his own language, so that, at the age of twenty-five, a diligent student has barely acquired the same amount of facility in reading and writing which is usually attained by an English child—using the twenty-six characters of his alphabet—at the age of ten; practically some four or five thousand characters suffice for average needs, and the convenience of "a system enabling those who speak mutually unintelligible idioms, to converse together, using the pencil instead of the tongue," caused the abandonment of an attempt to make nearer approach to an alphabetic system which was promoted by the Chinese Government some centuries ago.

In contrast to this, the Japanese, with that pliability which has helped to put them in the van of Oriental peoples, selected, as a result of contact with Buddhism, which came to them by way of China, certain signs from the wilderness of Chinese characters, and constituted these as their alphabet or irofa so called, on the acrologic principle (p. 104), from the names of its first signs, like our alphabet from alpha, beta. Their language being polysyllabic, involved the result that whatever signs were used must be syllabic, and hence the adoption of a syllabary was easy. But, of course, like all syllabaries, this has the defect of necessitating the use of that larger number of signs with which the alphabet dispenses. The origin of the Japanese syllabaries, of which there are two, dates from the end of the ninth century of our Lord. One, the Hirakana, derived from a cursive form of Chinese called the tsau or "grass" character, contains about three hundred syllabic sound-signs; the other, known as the Katakana, is derived from the kyai or "model" type of the Chinese character, and is the simpler of the two in having only a single character for each of the forty-seven syllabic sounds in the Japanese language. But neither demands detailed treatment here, since with the intrusion of the Roman alphabet among Western imports into Japan its substitution for the cumbrous syllabaries is probably only a matter of brief time, and the Japanese script may then take its place with the Maya and the Aztec as a graphic curiosity.

Chinese is the official script of Corea, but the lower classes use a phonetic alphabet which, in the judgment of some authorities, is derived from a cursive form of the Nâgari script of India, having, so it is thought, been introduced by Buddhist teachers. Both past and present times afford striking examples of the influence of religion in the diffusion of alphabets, missionaries obviously making use of their own alphabet in the translation of their sacred books into the language of their converts. Whatever connection there may have been between Corean and Indian scripts is not, however, traceable, owing to the changes in the former. But in truth we know little about the matter, and there is something to be said in support of an old tradition that King Se-jo, who reigned five hundred years ago, commanded his chief grammarian, Song Sammun, to devise an alphabet that should supersede the cumbersome Chinese; whereupon that scholar took the Tibetan characters as foundation, but as those were only consonantal, he turned to the ancient Chinese and transformed six of its simplest radicals into the Corean vowels, naming the vowels and consonants "mother" and "child" respectively. The letters were "bunched together" so as to look like the Chinese characters (Fig. 38), the purpose being "to facilitate the transliteration of the Chinese text in a parallel column." There is a curious tradition, reminding us of the Chinese legend of the origin of writing, that the Corean characters were suggested by the straight and oblique lattice-work of the native doors.

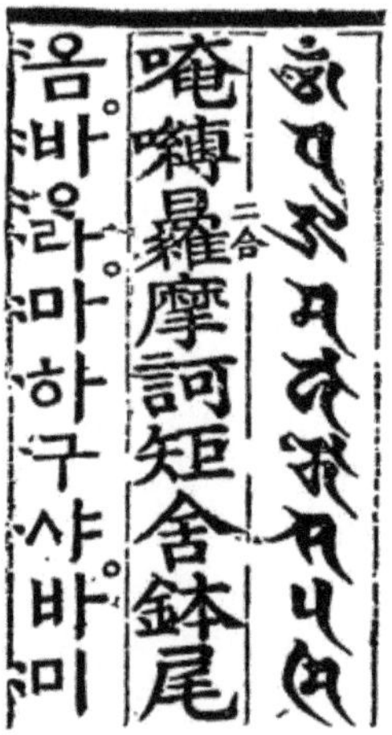

Fig. 38.—Chinese and Tibetan Triglot

CHAPTER V
CUNEIFORM WRITING

Thus far curiosity alone gives the stimulus to acquaintance with ancient scripts—a feeling of aloofness attending all that we learn of Chinese, Maya, and other systems having no historical connection (for the derivation of Chinese from pre-Babylonian writing is not proved) with those from which our alphabet is probably derived. With the story of these the real interest begins, because within some of them lie the sources of the alphabets of the civilised world, while all of them have borne a share in the preservation of intellectual and spiritual treasures, the loss of which would have arrested the progress of the vigorous sections of mankind.

Dealing first with those of Mesopotamia, a romance, not lacking excitement, gathers round the wedge-shaped or cuneiform characters (Lat. cuneus, "a wedge") inscribed on clay tablets and cylinders, and on the great monuments of Assyria, Babylon, and other Oriental empires of past renown. The very existence of these relics was forgotten for some sixteen hundred years, and when they were unearthed from the rubbish-heaps of centuries, no one dreamed that any serious meaning was to be attached to the fantastic angular-shaped characters which covered bricks and tablets. In 1621, Pietro della Valle, a Spanish traveller, visited the famous ruins of Persepolis, and he appears to have been the first to suspect that the arrow-headed signs were inscriptions, although he was unable to decipher them. He, however, made the shrewd observation that as the thick end of the supposed letters was never at the right but at the left of the oblique characters, the signs must have been written from left to right.

"Built on a great platform, artificially constructed for the purpose, which commands a wide plain, and has a lofty mountain shaped like an amphitheatre at its rear, the stranger ascends the spot by a magnificent staircase, or pair of staircases, which separate in opposite directions to meet at the summit. Here are the gigantic remains of several palaces, great porticos with winged bulls and reliefs representing, gods and princes. In the live rock of the mountains at the rear tombs have been hewn, evidently to receive the occupants of the palaces, and all the rocks and walls are covered with the cuneiform or arrow-headed inscriptions, consisting of very simple elements, which are nothing but thin wedges and angles

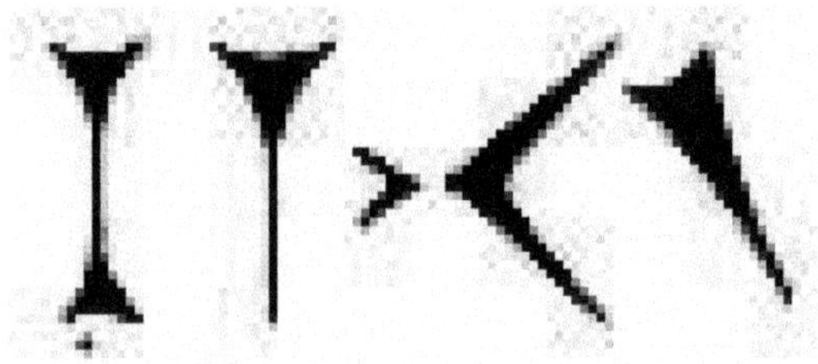

but with these elements combined in wonderful variety.... But no record of the language or its import had survived, and the ignorant inhabitants of the neighbourhood looked upon the texts with greater awe than they did the winged monsters that loomed over the plain. They were to them symbols of magic import, which, if duly pronounced, would unlock the hidden treasures guarded by the lions and the bulls." (Mahaffy's Prolegomena to Ancient History, p. 168.)

The savants of the seventeenth century were not "wiser in their generation" than the rude nomads who pitched their tents under the shadow of the stone monsters. Many years after Della Valle's visit the Oriental scholar, Hyde, in a book on the Ancient Persian Religion, soberly suggested that the signs were designed by some fantastic architect to show into how many combinations the same kind of stroke would enter. It is a wonder that he did not, with equal sobriety, suggest that they were related to the well-known Norman "hatchet-work." And so the guessing went on. One antiquary contended that they were talismanic signs; another that they were mystic formulæ of the priests, or astrological symbols of the old Chaldean star-worshippers; another saw in them a species of revealed digital language wherewith the Creator talked to Adam, whence the primitive speech of mankind was derived; while others conjectured them to be Chinese, or Samaritan, or Runic, or Ogam characters. Most fantastic of all, one ingenious theorist saw in them the action of numberless generations of worms!

But by the middle of the eighteenth century a sane school of investigators had found its leader. A great traveller, Carsten Niebuhr, father of the famous historian of early Rome, was the first to divine the true character of the inscriptions. He agreed with Della Valle that they were written from left to right, and he saw that they were made up of three different sets of characters, each meaning the same thing. But beyond showing, in his careful transcript published in 1764, that one of the three scripts was simpler in character than the others—all, as he assumed, being alphabetic varieties of one language—he could not go. The meaning still remained a mystery. Thirty years later, Münter, a Danish philologist, correctly guessed that the diagonal bar  , which occurred frequently, was a sign for the separation of words, and, next, he discovered the vowel signs, which, as distinct characters, are absent from the Hebrew and other Semitic languages. This was a great step towards final decipherment. Herodotus (i. 125, &c.) speaks of the Achæmenid dynasty of Persian kings who were the lords of Asia in the sixth and fifth centuries B.C. The ruins of Persepolis are identified as the remains of their palaces. Of this royal house the famous Darius was a member, and Herodotus tells how that monarch, "having gazed upon the Bosphorus, set up two pillars by it of white stone with characters cut upon them, on the one Assyrian and on the other Hellenic, being the names of all the nations which he was leading with him" (iv. 87). The engraving of the same inscription in two or more different languages (of course necessitated by making their decrees known to the various peoples whom they ruled) was thus shown to be a custom of the Persian kings.

Put upon the quest, a French scholar, M. de Sacy, born at Paris in 1758, copied some inscriptions of the Sassanid dynasty, which reigned in Persia A.D. 226-651. These were written in a known alphabet which is a mixture of Persian and Aramaic, called Pehlevi, and were shown by De Sacy to run in the following form:—"I, (M or W,) king of kings, son of (X,) king of kings, did thus and thus." Then, grouping together the several facts, came Dr. Georg Friedrich Grotefend, to formulate the theory that the Persepolitan inscriptions were written in three languages, and not three alphabets of one language, as Carsten Niebuhr had surmised. The recurrence of certain groups of characters led him to the inference that "the inscriptions were a fixed formula, only differing in the proper names." If these inscriptions began, like those read by De Sacy, with the formula, X, the king of kings, son of D, the king of kings, then it was clear that D was X's father; and, further, that D's father was not a king, because his name was not followed by that title, D being therefore the founder of a royal race. Now, Hystaspes, father of Darius, was not king, but satrap under Cambyses; and, joining his knowledge of history to his skill in philology, Grotefend found the key to the royal name. He lived for thirty years after this discovery, but added nothing to his triumph save "a fortunate guess of the name Nebuchadnezzar in one of the Assyrian inscriptions." Other decipherments followed; but it was reserved for the genius and industry of our countryman, the late Sir Henry Rawlinson, to discover the key whereby the ancient languages of Persia, Babylon, and Assyria can be read, and thus "a chapter of the world's history that had been well-nigh wholly lost made known to mankind." That eminent scholar in no wise exaggerated the importance of his work in claiming that its value in the interpretation of cuneiform writing is almost equal to that of the discovery of the Rosetta Stone in the interpretation of the hieroglyphic texts of Egypt (Archæologia, xxxiv. p. 75).

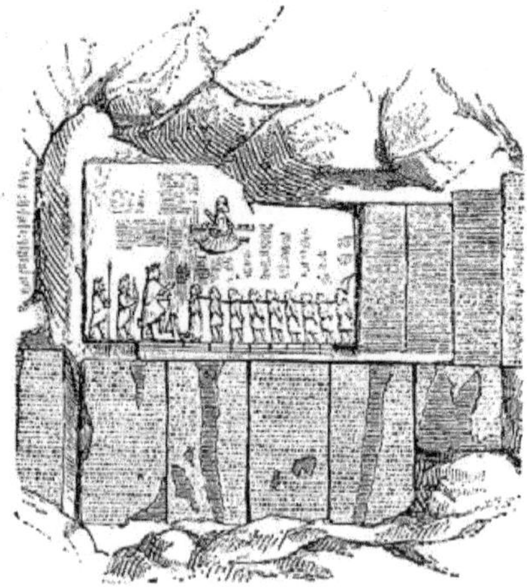

Fig. 39.—Rock Inscription at Behistun

The story of Rawlinson's achievement is warrant of the claim. About sixty years ago, being then a lieutenant, he was sent to Persia to drill the army of the Shah. His interest in Oriental history and antiquities was already keen, and he was glad to find himself in regions rich in materials the obscurity of whose meaning quickened inquiry. Among these was a trilingual inscription, dating from the early part of the sixth century B.C., cut on the face of a bare precipitous rock at Behistun, about twenty miles from Kirmanshah, a district abounding in monuments of the past (Fig. 39). At the risk of life and limb he climbed the face of the steep cliff to make copies of such portions of the inscriptions as were accessible with the means at his command, and after a series of efforts, continued at intervals through several years, he finally secured a complete transcript of so much of the writing as time had left uninjured. The inscription is in three languages—Babylonian, Mede or Scythian, and Persian—arranged in parallel columns containing above one thousand lines. It commemorates "the life and acts of Darius Hystaspes, his conquests, and the nations under his sway." Bas-reliefs portray that monarch, bow in hand, sitting with his feet on the prostrate usurper, Gaumates, while a train of nine rebel princes, whose names are inscribed above their effigies, stand before the "king of kings," chained together by the neck. Two of the monarch's soldiers are in the rear. Over Gaumates is written: "This is Gaumates, the Magian; he lied; he said, I am Smerdis, son of Cyrus." The same formula occurs over the heads of each of the nine captives. "This is (M); he lied; he said he was king of (N)." The inscription begins with a solemn invocation to Ormuzd, the old Persian god of light and purity, and passes on to detail the claim of Darius to the throne of the Achæmenids and the possessions of the Persian crown. It tells of the defeat of Smerdis, and of the revolt of Susiana, a province lying between Persia and Babylonia. "I sent thither an army, and the rebel Atrina was brought in chains before me; I slew him." The same story is narrated concerning other rebellious subjects. Of one Phraortes, it is told that his nose, ears, and tongue were cut off, and that he was "crucified at Ecbatana, together with his accomplices." Then the inscription proceeds:

> "King Darius saith: These countries rebelled against my power. By lies they were separated from me. The men thou seest here deceived my people. My army took them, according to my orders. King Darius saith: Oh, thou that shalt be king hereafter, see that thou art not guilty of deceit. Him that is wicked, judge as he should be judged, and if thou reignest thus thy kingdom will be great. King Darius saith: What I did, I did ever by the grace of Ormuzd. Thou that readest upon this stone my deeds, think not that thou hast been deceived, neither be thou slow to believe them. King Darius saith: Ormuzd be my witness that I have not spoken these things with lying lips." (Cf. Transactions of Royal Asiatic Society, 1844-46, 1851; also Life of Sir Henry Rawlinson, pp. 146, 153, 326.)

As Professor Mahaffy points out, the exact correspondence of this record, "especially in the many proper names it contains, with the names of persons and provinces described by Herodotus, is a convincing proof of the accuracy of the deciphering. It will give some notion of the style of the documents that have been preserved. It will also prove the accuracy of the accounts given by Herodotus and Xenophon of the character of the ancient Persians, in whom an honest love of truth and hatred of lies was the prominent feature—a feature which we justly honour more than any other in a nation, but in which most Oriental nations, and indeed the Greeks also, were woefully deficient." (Prolegomena, p. 186.)

Sir Henry Rawlinson's decipherment of the great inscription of Behistun did perhaps more than aught else to open the long-closed door to the secret of Mesopotamian culture. The Persian inscription is in a language which is the mother-tongue of modern Persian, and its meaning being discovered, the interpretation of the Medic or Scythic, and of the Babylonian, the oldest of the three, followed, while the several characters supplied a valuable object-lesson in the stages of the development of writing from the ideographic through the syllabic, and thence of approach to the alphabetic.

Cuneiform writing appears to have been originally inscribed upon a vegetable substance called likhusi, but the abundant clay of the alluvial country afforded material whose convenience and permanence brought it into general use. Upon this the characters were impressed by a reed or square-shaped stylus, the clay-books being afterwards baked or sun-dried. For inscriptions on stone or metal a chisel was used. The writing of the Assyrian scribes is often exceedingly minute, the tablets containing a mass of matter in a tiny space. The work was trying enough to sometimes require the use of a magnifying-glass, and among Sir Austin Layard's discoveries at Nineveh was that of a lathe-turned crystal lens which was probably used for the purpose. Obviously the substances chosen account for the angular form of the characters; as the dyer's hand is "subdued to what it works in," so the nature of the material in which the sculptor seeks to express his conceptions largely determines for him the limits of that expression. Phidias himself could not have produced his Pallas Athene from the stubborn granite of Syene; and, as the outcome of the Egyptian temperament, the sphinxes of the Nile valley might have worn a less relentless look had they been fashioned of the marble of Pentelicus. Much as the abrupt cuneiform character tends, however, to obscure the traces of its derivation, there are sufficing proofs that it is of pictographic origin, although no examples of picture-writing in Mesopotamia corresponding in primitiveness to those already given from barbaric sources have been discovered. In the linear Babylonian, as it is called, the hieroglyph for "sun" is a diamond-shaped figure  which later on became , and in the latest cuneiform, . Evidently the earliest sign was a circle, which could not be easily traced on the stone or clay, and hence appears as the angular character shown above. The annexed table, which is a copy of one supplied by Mr. Pinches to Professor Keane, and published in his admirable monograph, Man Past and Present, gives a set of typical examples of the derivation of cuneiform characters from the earliest known pictographs.

Evolution of the Akkadian Cuneiforms.

1000 B.C. and later.
About 2500 to 1500 B.C.
Oldest known line forms, 3000 B.C. and earlier.
"bird."
"sheep" (probably a sheep-fold).
"ox."
"to go," "to stand."
"hand."
"man."
"dagger."
"fish."
"reed."
"reed."
"corn" ("ear of corn").
"god," "heaven."
"constellation," "star."

As an illustration bearing upon the specimens set forth in the table we have the ideogram of Nineveh 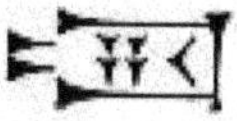. The archaic form of this character 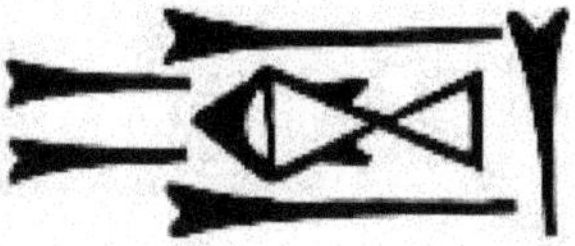 proves that it was compounded of the ideographic picture of a house, enclosing the ideogram of the fish , thus preserving record of the instructive fact that imperial Nineveh was at first, as its name implies (nun, "fish," is the name of the fourteenth letter of the Semitic alphabet), a collection of fishermen's huts (cf. Taylor, i. 41). The frequent mixture of old and new forms in cuneiform writings and the different values sometimes given to the same sign, have increased the difficult task of interpretation. As in the earlier stages of other languages, determinatives were used; e.g. all names of men were preceded by a single upright wedge, of countries by three horizontal wedges, and so on. But in the examples given in the table, the gradual conventionalising of the signs is seen, as in that for "ox," wherein the modification of the head and horns of the animal into the phonogram is obvious, while the Behistun inscription exhibits well-defined stages of approach to simplification. The cumbrous cuneiform which fills the third column has five hundred symbols, ideograms, phonograms, and homophones; the Medic, which occupies the second column, is written in ninety-six pure syllabic signs; while the Persian tells the same story in thirty-six alphabetic signs, four only of the primitive ideograms being retained. This survival of use of ideograms, it may be noticed in passing, has illustration among ourselves in many ways. As certain parts of the body, e.g. hand, foot, bosom (in Anglo-Saxon fæthem, i.e. "fathom," or the space of both arms extended), and forearm (Latin ulna, Anglo-Saxon eln, whence "ell"), became and remain standards of measurement, so it is with certain modes of reckoning. The digits, I, II, III, IIII (Latin digitus, "a finger") are unquestionably pictures of fingers, and Grotefend contends with good reason that V is a picture of the four fingers closed and the thumb extended, while X would represent the two hands, IV the subtraction and VI the addition of a finger. The use of a primitive decimal notation is widespread among barbaric peoples. In chess problems the several pieces are pictorially represented; in the planetary signs, ☿ is the caduceus or wand of Mercury; ♀ is the mirror of Venus, while the entomologist, in cataloguing his specimens, uses these symbols for the male and female respectively. In ♂ we have the shield and spear of Mars; in ♃ , the sign for Jupiter, the arm wields a thunderbolt; and the mower's scythe ♄ is the symbol of Saturn (connected with Latin sero, satum, "to sow"), the god of agriculture. The signs of the Zodiac, which were mapped out by the old Chaldeans, supply a still more cogent example. In the form in which they are depicted on the ancient temple of Denderah, in Egypt, there may be traced evidence of their primitive pictorial character, a character still recognised in the headings of the months in our almanacks (cf. Whitaker's), and to be detected in current symbols. For example, the curved horns of the ram survive in ♈ , the sign for Aries; the head and horns of the bull in ♉ , the sign for Taurus; the arrow and a portion of the bow in ♐ , the sign for Sagittarius; while, as Dr. Taylor points out, "the curious symbol ♑ is found to preserve the whole outline of Capricornus, the small circle being the head of the goat, with the forelegs below, and the body and tail extending to the left." Then in such entries in the almanack as " ☉ rises 4h. 25m.," " ☽ 11h. 54m.," " ● 10th 9.32 morn.," " ♃ 3420" in tables of the configuration of Jupiter's satellites, as also in the symbols for money, weights, measures, and so forth, the not wholly dispensed with picture-writing may be detected. The well-nigh vanished trade signs doubtless served a useful purpose as pictographs in guiding the illiterate to the shops of which they were in quest; and here and there the barber's pole with its spiral bandages reminds us of the phlebotomy of the past; the golden balls of the great financiers of Florence hang out from pawnbrokers' shops their delusive signal to the thriftless; while the "grasshopper" of Messrs. Martin, the "leather bottell" of Messrs. Hoare, and other remnants of goldsmiths' trade signs, remind us how many of these swung before the shops of Cheape and Lombard Street in olden time.

To return to the cuneiform. It will be remembered that in the case of the monosyllabic Chinese, with its dictionary of forty thousand words, the symbols of these are compounds of phonograms or sound-words with determinatives as keys to the precise meaning to be attached to the phonograms. Now the languages of the ancient peoples of the Euphrates valley are polysyllabic, and hence arose the necessity for signs denoting full syllables, both complex, "in which several consonants may be distinguished, or simple syllables composed of only one consonant and one vowel or vice versâ." (Maspero's Dawn of Civilization, p. 728.) And among the libraries of Babylon there were discovered a number of little grammatical documents on bricks, called syllabaria, where a list of characters is given, with the phonetic sign explained in simple syllables at one side, and, when used ideographically, at the other. When a syllabary had thus been adopted, the grouping into words was effected by combining the syllables. "But a polysyllabic language did not lend itself so readily as the Chinese monosyllabic to syllabism," and Halévy explains how the difficulty was met. It was met, at least in some degree, by the adoption of the principle of Acrology (Greek akron, "extreme" = at the top or start), i.e. by the choice of a name from the likeness which it suggested between the form of the letter and some familiar thing whose name began with the letter in question. This re-naming of letters by a word beginning with them occurred in the Egyptian, Russian, Runic, and other alphabets. For example, in Russian, the letter b is not called beta but buki, "a beech," while d has lost the old name of delta and acquired that of dobro, "an oak." In the Runic letters of our forefathers b is named beorc or "birch," and th "thorn," while the acrologic system comes nearer home to us in the old nursery rhymes: "A was an Archer, who shot at a frog; B was a Butcher, who had a big dog," &c.

Now this advance to syllabism had been effected, long before the Babylonians appear on the scene, by the older inhabitants of Mesopotamia, the Akkadians, or, more correctly, the Akkado-Sumerians, the Akkadians being settled on the highlands, and the Sumerians on the plains, of that region. The racial affinities of either are not determined, some ethnologists holding that they are of Finno-Turkic origin, others that they belong to the Tatar-Mongolic branch. Neither is it known at what period they immigrated into Chaldea, since at the dawn of history they are already merged in the Semitic conquering race. Some thousands of years B.C. Chaldea had been invaded by the people afterwards known as Babylonians, whose primitive home, in common with that of other Semites, as the Hebrews, Phœnicians, &c., is conjectured to have been in South Arabia. The Babylonians, mixing their blood with that of the subject peoples, settled as agriculturists on the rich alluvial lowlands, while an offshoot from them, the Assyrians, occupied the mountainous and wooded country to the north of the great rivers, keeping their Semitic purity of descent. These "Romans of the East," as they have been called, were soldiers and merchants, strong in the conviction that "trade follows the flag," and hence embarking in many an aggressive enterprise to beat the Phœnician and other rivals in commerce. But, resting on the sword alone, the Assyrian empire perished by the sword.

As for the Akkadians (using this term to include the pre-Semite inhabitants), they had passed the barbaric stage when they invaded Chaldea. They knew the use of metals: they were skilful architects, and; what was of importance in the marshy districts where dams and canals were indispensable, good engineers; their laws mark an advanced social organisation; their writing, as has been seen, had become syllabic; and their literature, besides recording the details of their daily life, supplies the key to a religion which profoundly influenced the Babylonians, and, through them, the Hebrews, ultimately affecting the whole of Christendom. That religion was a blend of higher and lower ideas. At base it was Shamanistic. Natural phenomena—sun, moon, stars, the earth, and so forth—were worshipped, but, as in all religions, that which touches man more closely in his affairs and relations has the firmer hold, and hence there was an active belief in magic, with its allied apparatus of charms, spells, and incantations. Side by side with formulæ embodying superstitions common to barbaric folk all the world over, we find penitential psalms, appeals to the great gods, and spiritual utterances, some of which are on a plane with Hebrew sacred poetry. All this body of literature, secular and sacred, made up the vast store of books in the libraries whose interpretation is one of the brilliant successes of modern scholarship, and whose contents bring home to us the priceless value of the art of writing to mankind.

Up to a recent date, the oldest known example of cuneiform writing was supplied by a porphyry cylinder seal of the Semite king, Sargon I., who flourished 3800 B.C. (Fig. 40). It bears this inscription:—"Sargon, King of the city of Akkad, to the Sun-god (Sarnas) in the city of Sippara I approached." It is this same king concerning whom a myth, which may have been the origin of the myth about the infant Moses in the bulrushes, is recorded on a tablet preserved, together with the seal, in the British Museum.

Fig. 40.—Cylinder Seal of Sargon I.

Another famous cuneiform relic is the Stele of the Vultures, a large portion of which is in the Louvre. It dates from about 4500 B.C., and besides its sculptured panels, one of which depicts vultures carrying away the heads of the slain in battle (whence its name), it records the victory of E-anna-du, priest-king of Sirpurra, over the "people of the land of the Bow," on the Elamite frontier, a tribute of corn being imposed on the conquered state. Other inscriptions testify that "in the fourth millennium before the Christian era art was fully developed, statues set up, the chariot used in war, silver and copper worked, weaving and the making of pottery known, and an elaborate system of calculation into thousands evolved." But the antiquity of these witnesses pales before that evidenced by the rubbish-mounds of the city of Nuffar or Nippur, in Northern Babylonia. Several records of Sargon I. were found among the thousands of tablets dug from the later deposits, but discoveries were made beneath these on which Dr. Peters, in reporting on the epigraphic material secured by Mr. Haynes, writes as follows:—"We found that Nippur was a great and flourishing city, and its temple, the temple of Bel, the religious centre of the dominant people of the world at a period as much prior to the time of Abraham as the time of Abraham is prior to our own day. We discovered written records no less than six thousand years old, and proved that writing and civilisation were then by no means in their infancy. Further than that, our explorations have shown that Nippur possessed a history extending backward of the earliest written documents found by us, at least two thousand years." (Nippur; the Narrative of the University of Pennsylvania's Expedition, vol. ii. p. 241.) Upon which Dr. Hilprecht comments: "I do not hesitate to date the founding of the temple of Bel and the first settlements in Nippur somewhere between 6000 and 7000 B.C., and possibly earlier." (Academy, 30th April 1898, p. 465.)

Fig. 41.—Tell-el-Amarna Tablet (circa 1450 B.C.)

Fig. 42.—First Creation Tablet

Although they are nearly five thousand years later, deeper interest attaches to the three hundred and twenty clay tablets, inscribed with the cuneiform character (Fig. 41), which were discovered in 1887 among the ruins of Tell-el-Amarna, the Arabic name of a village on the east bank of the Nile, about one hundred and eighty miles south of the once renowned city of Memphis. The village stands on the site of a city founded by Amenophis III., so that the date of the documents, among which are letters received by that king, is known to range from 1500 to 1450 B.C. Two of the tablets contain legends, and one gives a hymn to the war-god, but the larger number comprise communications passing between the kings of Egypt and the kings of Western Asia, many of them being docketed with the date and name of the sender written in Egyptian hieroglyph. One tablet from a Hittite prince is written in the old Akkadian tongue. They furnish valuable information upon the political and commercial relations between Egypt and Babylonia, and upon negotiations between the kings both for wives and subsidies. "Being all in the cuneiform character, they were unlikely to be readily deciphered at the Egyptian court. Hence it was the custom of the Babylonian kings to send interpreters with them, and reference is made to such messengers in several of the letters. But a scribe able to read and write the cuneiform was undoubtedly kept by the Pharaohs for purposes of translation and for inditing replies. Some of the tablets are copies of such replies, written in cuneiform, but retained for reference, just as we in the present day keep copies of important letters."

Fig. 43.—Deluge Tablet (Chaldean Epic) OBVERSE.

Fig. 44.—Deluge Tablet (Chaldean Epic) REVERSE.

The actual contents of the Tell-el-Amarna tablets are of secondary importance to the fact that cuneiform writing was in use in Palestine fifteen hundred years before Christ, and, therefore, that Babylonian myths and legends had, in all probability, circulated freely there centuries before the Book of Genesis took shape. Thus the legends of the Creation, the Fall, and the Deluge, the Chaldean origin of which is established (Figs. 42, 43, 44), "can very well have existed in Palestine at the time it was invaded by the Israelites, who would have learned them from the people they subdued, and would have found plenty of time to modify them into the forms in which they appear in Hebrew literature." (The Witness of Assyria, p. 11, by Chilperic Edwards.)

CHAPTER VI
EGYPTIAN HIEROGLYPHICS

With the foregoing references to some of the most venerable documents that have yet come to light, we may leave Assyria for Egypt, no longer a land of marvel and of mystery, with its past hidden as the sources of the great river of which that land is "the gift" were long hidden. For the discovery of the key to that past, and of the vast waters that feed the Nile, alike lie within the present century. Till then the veil of Isis hung over the significance of the inscriptions on coffin, sepulchral box, stele, tomb, obelisk, and temple, and over the interpretation of characters written on papyri rolls centuries before the foundations of Athens were laid. Of these records, be it noted, Death, which sweeps away man and the memory of him from his fellows, has been more than aught else—in Egypt, and indeed, all the world over, but notably in Egypt—the preserver. And this because there all that appertained to the departed was guarded with the most jealous care. The tomb, as often elsewhere, was modelled on the plan of the house, and supplied with utensils, food, and drink, or adorned with the painted representations of these things on the walls, for the needs of the ka, or double, sahn, or spirit, or some other of the eight Egyptian ontological divisions of the individual.

Like the other pictographic systems already surveyed, the Egyptian interests us because it has preserved the traces of its origin, adding its "cloud of witnesses" to the identity of the several stages of development marking the scripts of all literate peoples. Until very recently, its chief interest lay in the belief that it is the parent of the family of alphabets of the civilised world; but, as will be shown later on, the theory is no longer tenable. Although the earliest known examples of Egyptian hieroglyphs (Greek hieros, "sacred," and glypho, "to carve," so called in the belief that they were used solely by the priests) contain alphabetic characters, they have come down as highly elaborated types of picture-writing, the changes in which during the long period covered by the records being so slight that, to cite Professor Whitney, "it is like a language which has never forgotten the derivations of its words, or corrupted their etymological form, however much it may have altered its meaning." Therefore, although the Egyptians had developed alphabet-signs five thousand years B.C. they never advanced to the stage of their sole and independent use, partly because of the conservative instincts of the race, which, fostering veneration for the old, was reluctant to alter anything, and partly because, as Professor Flinders Petrie has pointed out, their "treatment of everything was essentially decorative, the love of form and drawing being in Egypt a greater force than amongst any other ancient people. Babylon and China, from want of sufficient artistic taste, allowed their pictorial writing to sink into a mere string of debased and conventional forms; the Egyptians, on the contrary, preserved the purely pictorial and artistic character of their hieroglyphs to the end. The hieroglyphs were a decoration in themselves; their very position in the sentence was subordinate to the decorative effect. The Egyptian could not be guilty of the barbarism seen on some of the Assyrian sculpture, where inscriptions were scrawled right across the work without regard to design. So far was this idea carried that many words or ideas were represented by two distinct characters, one wide and the other narrow and deep, so that the harmony of the design should not be broken by an unsuitable element. The result was that the Egyptians were rewarded by having the most beautiful writing in the world." (Egyptian Decorative Art, p. 4.)

This writing exists in three groups of characters (Fig. 45): (a) Hieroglyphic, (b) Hieratic, (c) Demotic. The demotic is derived from the hieratic, and the hieratic from the hieroglyphic.

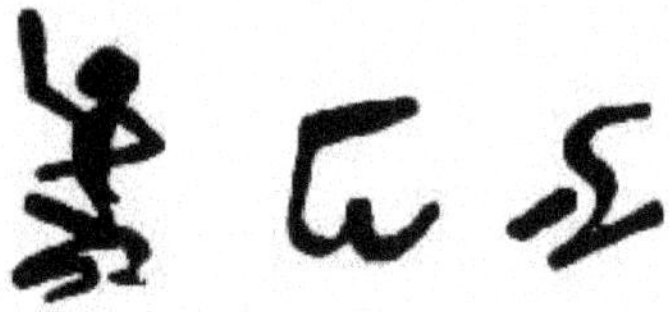

Fig. 45.—Hieroglyphic, Hieratic, and Demotic Signs for Man

(a) Pictogram, ideogram, and phonogram—in other words, signs representative of word, idea, and sound—make up the seventeen hundred hieroglyphs which, in the older signs, preserve the traces of their origin in rude picture-writing. They were chiselled on stone of various kinds, cut or painted on wood or plaster, and written on papyrus or skin; the characters being arranged in vertical columns.

With the quickened zeal of modern excavators discoveries come apace, so that before these words are printed, some additional find, throwing all others into the shade, may come to light. Such, for example, would be the production of epigraphic evidence as to the sojourn and oppression of the Israelites in Egypt, and their escape from that "house of bondage." For a long time the earliest known example of hieroglyphic writing which the Gizeh and Ashmodean Museums could show (each institution possessing fragments of the relic) was a mutilated stele or monumental tablet to the memory of Shera, a priest or grandson of Sent, the fifth king of the Second Dynasty, which, adopting Professor Flinders Petrie's chronology, flourished about four thousand five hundred years B.C. In this record three alphabetic characters are employed to spell that monarch's name. But in November 1897, Dr. Borchardt reported the important discovery that the royal tomb found by M. de Morgan in the spring of that year at Nagada, situated opposite Coptos, a little north of Thebes, is that of Menes, the founder of the First Dynasty, whose date Professor Flinders Petrie fixes at 4777 B.C., "with a possible error of a century." Calcined remains of the body are now in the Gizeh Museum, and, among other objects, the broken fragments of an ivory plaque which, when joined, showed the ka name of Aha (the ka being the "double" or "other self" of the deceased which abode with the mummy), and, attached thereto, the name MN = Menes, borne by the Pharaoh during his lifetime. Assuming that Dr. Borchardt's interpretation is accepted by Egyptologists, it proves that the hieroglyphic system of writing was then already fully developed. It may be remarked, incidentally, that among the remains of the pre-dynastic race discovered by Professor Flinders Petrie in 1895, in the district north of Thebes, no hieroglyphs or traces of other writing were found. There was evidence of knowledge of metals, but not of the potter's wheel. It therefore seems probable that writing came in with the First Dynasty, which, according to M. de Morgan, was descended from Chaldean Semites.

But more interesting, for the light thrown on early Egyptian thought, than inscriptions on stele or plaque are the copies of portions of the sacred literature entitled "Chapters of the Coming Forth by Day," and also the "Chapters of Making Strong the Beatified Spirit," but commonly known as the Book of the Dead. This venerable embodiment of human conceptions about an after life, and of human hope and consolation this side the grave, contains the hymns, prayers, and magic formulæ against all opposing foes and evil spirits, to be recited by the dead Osiris (the soul was conceived to have such affinity with the god Osiris as to be called by his name) in his journey to Amenti, the underworld that led to the Fields of the Blessed. It lies outside both our scope and space to give an account of the contents of the several chapters, and, fortunately, the entire text, translated by Dr. Wallis Budge, with admirable facsimiles of illustrations, is within the reach of a moderate purse. But one curious and prominent feature should have reference, because it shows the persistence of barbaric ideas about names as integral parts of things. (On this subject, see the author's Tom Tit Tot; an Essay on Savage Philosophy in Folk-Tale, 1898.) The Osiris has not only to be able to recite the names and titles of the gods, but of every part of the boat, "from truck to keel," as the nautical phrase goes, in which he desires to cross the great river flowing to Amenti. And then, before he can enter the Hall of the Two Truths—that is, of Truth and Justice, where the god Osiris and the forty-two judges of the dead are seated—the jackal-headed Anubis requires him to tell the names of every part of the doors, posts, and woodwork generally. These correctly given, the soul declares its innocence in language whose moral tone has never been surpassed, while it throws a light on the virtues and vices of old Egyptian society which makes clear how poor a guide to the past are its monuments compared with its literature.

The age of the composition of this remarkable book is unknown. But so old is it that the earliest copies we possess show that when they were made, some six thousand years ago, the exact meaning of parts of the text had become obscure to the transcribers. Fragments of it have been found in those ancient tombs, the Pyramids; chapters or long extracts were written on stone and wooden coffins; but after the expulsion of the Hyksos, or Shepherd Dynasty, by the kings of Thebes, about 1580 B.C., papyrus came more into use for the purpose.

One of the most superbly-illustrated examples is that known as the Papyrus of Ani, belonging to what is called the Theban recension of the text, which was much used from the Eighteenth to the Twentieth Dynasty (1587-1060 B.C.). It will suffice, as evidence of the magical qualities attributed to the written word, to quote the following from the seventy-second chapter, as translated into sonorous English by Dr. Wallis Budge:—

> "If this writing be known (by the deceased) upon earth, and this chapter be done into writing upon (his) coffin, he shall come forth by day in all the forms of existence which he desireth, and he shall enter into (his) place, and be not rejected. Bread and ale and meat shall be given unto Osiris, the scribe Ani upon the altar of Osiris ... there shall wheat and barley be given unto him; there shall he flourish as he did upon earth, and he shall do whatsoever pleaseth him, even as do the gods who are in the underworld, for everlasting millions of ages, world without end."

Under Dr. Wallis Budge's editorship, the Ani papyrus has recently been supplemented by the issue of facsimiles and translations of papyri and other texts connected with the Book of the Dead. Among these is a Book of Breathings, written in a late hieratic, and dating from late pre-Christian times. It contains a ritual to be said by the priest for or over the dead, and teaches belief in a resurrection of the body and a state of material bliss on earth. "Thy soul shall live," and, so runs the text, "thy corruptible body shall burst into life, and thou shalt never decay." ... "Grant that his soul may go into every place wheresoever it would be, and let him live upon earth for ever and ever."

Up to a point the story of Egyptian writing illustrates the stages of development of writing generally so clearly that its recital, even at the cost of some repetition, will be helpful, and the more so as it falls into line with the story of other scripts.

"It goes without saying" that the representation of an object was a simple matter enough, the rudest draughtsmanship sufficing for a picture that should tell its own meaning at a glance. But as soon as the need arose to graphically express ideas, for example, such as vice and virtue, time and space, health and sickness, symbolism came in. To the illustrations of this supplied by the scripts already dealt with may be added a few examples from Egyptian ideography, into which, at the stage that we first meet it, the whole system of hieroglyphics may be said to have become modified. The bee was a symbol of kingship and also of industry; a roll of papyrus denoted knowledge; an ostrich feather, justice, because these feathers were supposed to be of equal length; a palm branch, one year, because that tree was popularly believed to put forth a fresh branch every new moon—although, as Mr. Gliddon suggests, a more plausible reason is in the annual cutting of the lower leaves close to the trunk. The ideograph for a priest was a jackal—not, as may be cynically hinted, because of his "devouring widows' houses," but because of his watchfulness; for a mother, a vulture, because that bird was believed to nourish its young with its own blood. Thirst was represented by a calf running towards water; power by a brandished whip; and battle by two arms, the one holding a shield and the other a javelin. Among the Dakotah Indians combat is indicated by two arms pointed at each other. The ideograph for night, a star pendant from a curve, is like the Ojibwa; while among the ancient Mexicans night was represented by a semicircle with eyes, as stars, attached to it. Signs for hunger, thirst, supplication, and so forth, among both Innuit Indian and ancient Egyptian—as indeed many other signs among peoples, both in the old world and the new, whose writing has not reached a purely phonetic stage—have that correspondence to be expected when things common to all men are graphically represented (Fig. 46). Running water, for example, remains necessarily a pictograph, but water depicted in connection with rites represents, by one symbol or another, the varying nature of the latter. Both in Egypt and Mexico it is represented flowing from a vessel, the Egyptian ideograph having a kneeling figure with arms uplifted, as if in adoration or gratitude. There appears, also, some resemblance between the symbol for negation between these two, but this has the doubt attaching to all metaphysical interpretation of signs.

Fig. 46.—Comparative Ideographs

Obviously, this presentment of ideas through graphic designs into which metaphor often bordering on enigma had to be read, implied good memories and clear grasp of association on the part of the interpreter. Any doubt or ambiguity, with resulting confusion, as to the meaning of the symbol, rendered it worse than useless. Hence the addition of "determinants," concerning which something was said when treating of the Chinese script (see p. 85). These are of two classes—the special and more numerous, whose use was confined to one word or idea; and the general, numbering about two hundred, which, like the Chinese "keys," refer to whole groups of words.

But ideas have to be arranged in sentences, and these are made up of nouns, adjectives, verbs, and other parts of speech for which symbolism, however ingenious, can make no provision. Moreover, while the characters are limited in their application, the ideas to be expressed graphically are ever growing, and hence, in course of time, there are not enough symbols "to go round." A way of escape opened itself, and thereby led to an invention undreamed of, when recourse was had to the use of pictures of things which were different in sense, but the names of which had the same sound; in other words, to the pictorial pun known as the rebus (see p. 79). As an amusing instance of the formation of a compound phonogram out of syllabic signs, Canon Taylor quotes from an inscription of Ptolemy XV. at Edfu, in which, as he says, "it seems not impossible to detect a faint flavour of ancient Egyptian humour. The name of lapis lazuli was khesteb. Now the word khesf meant 'to stop,' and the syllable teb, 'a pig.' Hence the rebus 'stop-pig' was invented to express graphically the name of lapis lazuli, which is figured by the picture of a man stopping a pig by pulling at its tail." Probably the Canon is right, but in western lands that action is often intended to make the pig move on. Another example of the rebus occurs in the name of Osiris, which in Egyptian is Hesiri (Wallis Budge gives it as Ausir). The god, on this showing, is represented, presumably, by a figure on a seat, hes, and by an eye, iri. But with the constant revision of interpretations by Egyptologists, it behoves us to quote with caution. There is a stock illustration as to the adoption of the supposed picture of a lute (used by the Egyptian scribes to denote "excellence"), as a phonogram to express the word nefer, "good." But it seems that what was thought to be a lute is the picture of a heart and windpipe!

At last, we know not when, and we cannot, speaking of Egypt alone, guess where, there dawned upon some mind the fact that all the words which men uttered are expressed by a few sounds. Hence, what better plan than to select from the big and confused mass of ideograms, phonograms, and all their kin, a certain number of signs to denote, unvaryingly, certain sounds?

That was the birth of the ALPHABET, one of the greatest and most momentous triumphs of the human mind. The earliest phonograms represented syllables, not individual letters, the distinguishing signs for vowels and consonants being of yet later introduction; in fact, some alphabets, notably the Hebrew and other Semitic, have no true vowels, but only distinguishing marks, diacritical points as they are called, to denote them. To recapitulate, we have 1, picture-writing; 2, ideograms; 3, phonograms representing words; 4, phonograms representing syllables; 5, alphabetic characters. From their four hundred verbal phonograms and syllabic signs the Egyptians of a remote age—for it is literally true "that the letters of the alphabet are older than the Pyramids"—appear to have selected at the outset forty-five symbols for alphabetic use, but the rare occurrence or special use of some of these caused a further reduction to twenty-five letters. "All that remained to be done was to take one simple step—boldly to discard all the non-alphabetic elements, at once to sweep away the superfluous lumber, rejecting all the ideograms, the homophones, the polyphones, the syllables, and the symbolic signs to which the Egyptian scribes so fondly clung, and so to leave revealed in its grand simplicity the nearly perfect alphabet, of which, without knowing it, the Egyptians had been virtually in possession for almost countless ages." (Taylor, i. 68.) That step they never took, but continued the use of eye-pictures side by side with that of ear-pictures, instead of passing to the use of fixed signs for certain sounds.

(b) The cursive writing known as Hieratic was an abridged and conventionalised form of the hieroglyphic. The use of the latter became mainly restricted to monumental and kindred purposes, while the hieratic was employed by the priests in copying literary compositions, notable among which was the Book of the Dead, papyrus being the material most commonly used. This was made from the byblus hieraticus or Cyperus papyrus, a plant which flourished in the marshy districts of the Nile. There it has long been extinct, and is now found only in Sicily. It would seem to have served as many useful purposes to the ancient Egyptians as the bamboo serves to-day to the Chinese and other Orientals. "The roots were used for firewood, parts of the plant were eaten, and other and coarser parts were made into paper, boats, ropes, mats, &c." In preparing it for writing material, the outer rind was removed and the pith then cut into strips; which were laid side by side, with another set of strips across them fastened by a thin solution of gum, thus forming a sheet, which was pressed, dried in the sun, and polished to a smooth surface. The sheets were often joined to make a roll, which was sometimes above one hundred feet long and varied in width from six to seventeen inches. The finest papyri of the Book of the Dead are about fifteen inches wide, and, when they contain a tolerably large number of chapters, are from eighty to ninety feet long. Dipping his reed, which was either bruised at the end to make it brush-like, or cut, pen-like, to a point, in the ink-wells of his stone, wooden, or sometimes ivory palette, which was often dedicated to the god Thoth, "lord of divine words," the professional scribe wrote the text in varying colours, chiefly black or red, but also in other tints imitative of the subject dealt with, as blue for sky, yellow for woman, and so forth.

The earliest known specimen of hieratic writing is a papyrus containing chronicles of the reign of King Asa, whose date, according to a moderate estimate of Egyptian chronology, is about 3580 B.C. To the same period the most perfect literary work which has come down to us is usually assigned, although the copy preserved in the Bibliothèque Nationale in Paris, whither it was brought by M. Prisse d'Avennes from Thebes, seems to have been written between 2700 and 2500 B.C. This valuable relic, commonly known after its donor as the Papyrus Prisse, is entitled the "Precepts of Ptah-Hetep," and its contents justify the judgment of Dr. Wallis Budge, that "if all other monuments of the great civilisation of Egypt were wanting, it alone would show the moral worth of the Egyptians, and the high ideals of man's duties which they had formed nearly five thousand five hundred years ago."

(c) The Demotic or Enchorial characters preserve but slight traces of their derivation from picture-writing. As the term hieratic (Greek hieratikos, sacerdotal) denotes the class by whom that writing was used, so the terms demotic (Greek demotikos, of the people) and enchorial (Greek enchōrios, of the country) denote that this writing was in popular use, being adapted to the purposes of daily life. It appears to have come into use about 900 B.C., and so continued till the fourth century of our era. It has been shown that in the time of Darius and other rulers of the Achæmean dynasty, proclamations and documents of general importance were set forth in three languages—Babylonian, Medic, and Persian.

So, in the time of the Ptolemies, who inherited the Egyptian possessions of Alexander the Great and ruled in the Nile Valley till it fell under the sway of Rome, all matters of public importance were made known in hieroglyphic, demotic, and Greek characters. The hieroglyphic was called the "writing of divine words"; the demotic, "writing of letters"; and the Greek, "writing of the Greeks."

CHAPTER VII
THE ROSETTA STONE

The expressions given above occur on the famous Rosetta Stone, an inscribed slab of black basalt, which has proved to be of priceless value in supplying the key to the interpretation of Egyptian hieroglyphs, thus fulfilling a purpose corresponding to that of the Behistun rock inscriptions in the interpretation of cuneiform writing. The slab—which is preserved in the British Museum—takes its name from its discovery among the ruins of a fort near the Rosetta mouth of the Nile, where it was found by a French officer in 1799. On the capitulation of Alexandria to the British, the stone, whose importance had been detected by the savants attached, by the foresight of Napoleon, to his expedition, came by good fortune under the charge of Sir William Hamilton, whose interest in Egyptian antiquities was keen. It is not perfect, but enough has survived to suffice for decipherment of the general tenor of the inscriptions. Speculation as to the meaning of the hieroglyphs had been rife for centuries, for although they remained in use one hundred and fifty years after the Ptolemies began to reign (305 B.C.), and although the names of Roman emperors were written in them as late as the third century A.D., only a few among the classical writers whose works we possess have anything of value to say on the matter. It was not until the early decades of the present century that the ingenuity of two Egyptologists, Young and Champollion, working independently (as, years later, Adams and Leverrier worked at the problem of the discovery of Neptune), wrested their secret from the hieroglyphs. Honour lies only in lesser degree with some immediate predecessors, among them Zoëga, who rightly conjectured that the oblong rings enclosed royal names, because these "cartouches," as they are called, appeared above the series of sitting figures in temple sculptures; and Akerblad, who published an alphabet of the demotic characters on the Rosetta Stone.

Dr. Thomas Young was a very remarkable man. Born of Quaker parents in 1773, he gave his youth to literature, languages, and mechanics, and at thirty won the Fellowship of the Royal Society, having two years before then accepted the Professorship of Natural Philosophy at the Royal Institution. Made easy in circumstances by a legacy from a relative, he applied himself yet more strenuously to physics and philology. The result of his labours in the one was the discovery of the undulatory nature of light (which has its analogy in sound-waves), in opposition to Newton's corpuscular or emission theory; and, in the other, a partial decipherment of the demotic characters, and correct identification of the names of a few of the Egyptian gods—Rā, Nut, Thoth, Osiris, Isis, and Nephthys—and of the names Ptolemy and Berenice. He died in 1829.

Jean François Champollion, of whom Dr. Wallis Budge speaks as "the immortal discoverer of a correct system of decipherment of Egyptian hieroglyphics," was born in 1790. Like Young, he betook himself early to the study of languages, and at the age of thirteen was "master of a fair knowledge of Hebrew, Syriac, and Chaldee." In his twenty-second year he became Professor of Ancient History to the Faculty of Letters at Grenoble, and, with a certain impulse to the quest given by acquaintance with the labours of Young and others, he revised their system and developed his own, making tours to the museums of Turin, Rome, and Naples for the study of papyri, and passing thence to Egypt, where he secured a large body of materials. Death overtook him in 1832, but not before he had accomplished the chief aim of his life in demonstrating that the hieroglyphic characters are partly pictures of objects and partly signs of sounds.

Although the Rosetta Stone was the base of decipherment of Egyptian hieroglyphics, the success following Champollion's labours is largely due to the discovery of a small obelisk in the island of Philæ. This obelisk was said to have been fixed in a socket bearing a Greek inscription containing a petition of the priests of Isis at Philæ, addressed to Ptolemy, to Cleopatra his sister, and to Cleopatra his wife. The hieroglyphic inscription upon the obelisk itself included certain characters within a cartouche which were identical with those within the only cartouche occurring on the Rosetta Stone. Here, then, was a clue, which was the more easily followed up because the names of Ptolemy and Cleopatra have, in the Greek, certain letters in common which could be used for comparison with the hieroglyphics. "If the characters which are similar in these two names express the same sound in each cartouche, their purely phonetic character is at once made clear," and the recovery of the Egyptian alphabet was only a question of time (Figs. 47, 48, 49).

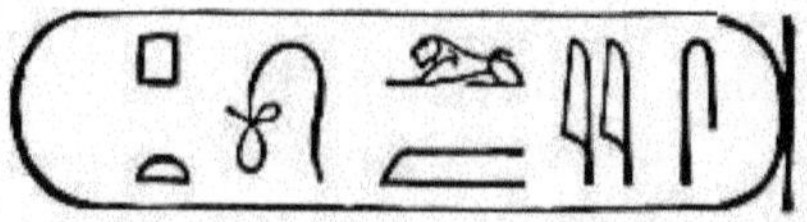

Fig. 47.—Ptolemy

Fig. 48.—CLEOPATRA

Fig. 49.—KAISARS (CÆSAR) A. TAKRTR (AUTOKRATOR)

The Rosetta Stone is inscribed with fragments of fourteen lines of hieroglyphics, thirty-two lines of demotic, and fifty-four lines of Greek. These have for their subject-matter a decree of the priesthood assembled at Memphis in honour of Ptolemy V. Epiphanes, King of Egypt, B.C. 195. They set forth the beneficent deeds of that monarch, in his consecration of revenues of silver and corn to the temples, his abolition of certain taxes and reduction of others, his grant of privileges to the priests and soldiers, and his undertaking at his own cost, in the eighth year of his reign, when the Nile rose to so great a height as to flood all the plains, the task of damming it and directing the overflow of its waters into proper channels, to the great gain and benefit of the agricultural classes. Besides his remissions of taxes, he gave handsome gifts to the temples, and subscribed to the various ceremonies connected with public worship. In return for these gracious acts, the priests assembled at Memphis decreed that a statue of the king should be set up in a conspicuous place in every temple of Egypt, and inscribed with the names and titles of "Ptolemy, the saviour of Egypt." Royal apparel was to be placed on the statues, and ceremonies were to be performed before them three times a day. It was also decreed that a gilded wooden shrine, containing a gilded wooden statue of the king, should be placed in each temple, and that these were to be carried out with the shrines of the other kings in the great panegyrics. It was also decreed that ten golden crowns of a peculiar design should be made and laid upon the royal shrine; that the birthday and coronation day of the king should be celebrated each year with great pomp and show; that the first five days of the month of Thoth should each year be set apart for the performance of a festival in honour of the king; and, finally, that a copy of this decree, engraved upon a tablet of hard stone in hieroglyphic, demotic, and Greek Characters, should be set up in each of the temples of the first, second, and third orders, near the statue of the ever-living Ptolemy. Dr. Wallis Budge adds that "the Greek portion of the inscriptions appears to be the original document, and the hieroglyphic and demotic versions merely translations of it." (The Mummy, pp. 110, 111.)

As the principle of interpretation is the same for all the inscriptions, and as the key to that interpretation is knowledge of one of the languages in which the inscription occurs, brief reference to another historical tablet often bracketed with the Rosetta Stone will suffice. This is known as the Stele of Canopus, which also bears inscriptions in hieroglyphic, demotic, and Greek. It is about half a century earlier than the Rosetta Stone, and was set up at Canopus in the ninth year of the reign of Ptolemy III. to record a decree made by the priesthood there assembled in honour of the king. It recites acts similar in their beneficent character to those recounted of Ptolemy V., and decrees what honours shall be paid him and his consort Berenice, whose famous hair, dedicated in the temple of Arsinoë at Zephyrium in gratitude for Ptolemy's safe return from his Syrian expedition, was said to have been metamorphosed into the constellation known as Coma Berenices.

CHAPTER VIII
EGYPTIAN WRITING IN ITS RELATION TO OTHER SCRIPTS

The interpretation of the Egyptian hieroglyphics being thus settled once and for all, the next problem to be attacked was their relation, if any, to the sound-signs whence are derived the alphabets of the civilised world. We travel backwards along clearly-marked lines from our alphabet to the Roman, and thence to the Greek, which tradition attributed to the Phœnicians. Herodotus says upon this matter: "Now these Phœnicians who came with Cadmos, of whom were the Gephyraians, brought in among the Hellenes many arts when they settled in this land of Bœotia, and especially letters, which did not exist, as it appears to me, among the Hellenes before this time; and at first they brought in those which are used by the Phœnician race generally, but afterwards, as time went on, they changed with their speech the form of the letters also. During this time the Ionians were the race of Hellenes who dwelt near them in most of the places where they were; and these, having received letters by instruction of the Phœnicians, changed their form slightly and so made use of them, and in doing so they declared them to be called 'phœnicians,' as was just, seeing that the Phœnicians had introduced them into Hellas. Also, the Ionians from ancient time call paper 'skins,' because formerly, paper being scarce, they used skins of goats and sheep; nay, even in my own time many of the Barbarians wrote on such skins" (v. 58).

Pliny, in his Natural History (v. 12, 13), gives the credit of the invention of the alphabet to the Phœnicians, and other ancient authors repeat what must have been an old tradition. The honesty of these writers is unimpeachable, however much their competency may be questioned; and no slight confirmation of their testimony appears, in the judgment of many modern scholars, to be furnished by the correspondence in number, name (the sibilants s and z excepted), and order, although not in form, between the letters of the Greek and the Semitic alphabets. "In default of further evidence, the very word ALPHABET," Canon Taylor remarks, "might suffice to disclose the secret of its origin. It is obviously derived from the names of the two letters alpha and beta, which stand at the head of the Greek alphabet, and which are plainly identical with the names aleph and beth borne by the corresponding Semitic characters. These names, which are meaningless in Greek, are significant Semitic words, aleph denoting an 'ox,' and beth a 'house.'" The following table shows the names and order of the Greek and Semitic letters, the Hebrew being selected as the type of a

Semitic alphabet, because it is more familiar than any other (cf. Taylor's History of the Alphabet, vol. i. p.75).

HEBREW.			GREEK.			
	Name.	**Meaning.**				**Name**
א	Aleph	ox	Α	α		Alpha
ב	Beth	house	Β	β	ϐ	Beta
ג	Gimel	camel	Γ	γ		Gamma
ד	Daleth	door	Δ	δ		Delta
ה	He	window	Ε	ε		Epsilon
ו	Vau	hook		(Vau	—	obsolete)
ז	Zayin	weapons	Ζ	ζ		Zeta
ח	Cheth	fence	Η	η		Eta
ט	Teth	serpent?	Θ	ϑ	θ	Theta
י	Yod	hand	Ι	ι		Iota
ך	Kaph	palm of hand	Κ	ϰ		Kappa
ל	Lamed	ox-goad	Λ	λ		Lambda
ם	Mem	waters	Μ	μ		Mu
ן	Nun	fish	Ν	ν		Nu
ס	Samekh	post	Ξ	ξ		Xi
ע	'Ayin	eye	Ο	ο		Omicron
ף	Pe	mouth	Π	π		Pi
ץ	Tsade	javelin?		(San	—	lost)
ק	Qoph	knot?		(Koppa	—	obsolete)
ר	Resh	head	Ρ	ϱ		Rho
ש	Shin	teeth	Σ	σ	ς	Sigma
ת	Tau	mark	Τ	τ		Tau
			Υ	υ		Upsilon *

Φ	φ	Phi *
Χ	χ	Chi *
Ψ	ψ	Psi *
Ω	ω	Omega *

*"of later origin"

Assuming the theory of the Phœnician origin of the alphabet to be established, the next question is, was that alphabet an independent invention, or was it adapted from another set of characters? As has been seen, all evidence goes to show that sound-signs have been derived from pictographs, and, if the Phœnician script be no exception to this, search must be made for its earlier forms. Tradition asserted that "the Phœnicians did not claim to be themselves the inventors of the art of writing, but admitted that it was obtained by them from Egypt." So says Eusebius, and the same tradition has currency among classic authorities from Plato to Tacitus, while the fact of the active intercourse which long prevailed between Phœnicia and Egypt goes far in its support. The Phœnicians were of Semitic race, "dwelling in ancient time, as they themselves report, upon the Erythrean Sea" (i.e. in the neighbourhood of the Red Sea and the Persian Gulf), "and thence they passed over and dwelt in the country along the sea coast of Syria; and this part of Syria and all as far as Egypt is called Palestine" (Herodotus, vii. 89). But of their origin and primitive migrations, in truth, little is known. Tyre, whose king, Hiram, gave Solomon aid in the building of his famous temple, and Sidon, are familiar names in the Bible, but that of the "Phœnicians" does not once occur, reference to them being probably included in the term "Canaanite." Professor Huxley, always felicitous in his phrases as he was supreme in exposition, aptly called them the "colossal pedlars" of the ancient world. The narrow strip of Syrian seaboard which they occupied when we first meet them in history was a meeting-place between East and West, and the nursery of a maritime enterprise which looms large in history. Their ships traded westward beyond the Pillars of Hercules, and eastward to the Indian Ocean; their colonists settled on both shores of the Mediterranean, on the Euxine, and were scattered over Asia Minor. Like the Romans, the Phœnicians had little creative instinct. Designing or discovering little, but skilfully manufacturing and circulating much, they were distributors of the wares of their own and neighbouring countries, and founded emporia in many a city of the ancient world, as e.g. at Memphis, "round about whose sacred enclosure, on that side of the temple of Hephaistos which faces the north wind, dwell

Phœnicians of Tyre, this whole region being called the camp of the Tyrians," or, as we should say, the Tyrian quarter (Herodotus, ii. 112).

Obviously, one of the pressing needs of a people thus brimful of commercial activity, to whom "time was money," would be some swift and concise mode of record of transactions. Hence the supersession or abbreviation of cumbrous and elaborated characters, with their apparatus of determinatives, ideograms, and the like, by a simple "shorthand" sort of script. But of what characters? Influenced partly by the traditions already referred to, partly by the fact of the intimate relations between Phœnicia and Egypt, and doubtless by that principle of development the application of which was extending in all directions, a French Egyptologist, Emanuel de Rougé, read a paper on the history of the alphabet before the Académie des Inscriptions in 1859 (the year of publication of Darwin's Origin of Species), which, in the judgment of many scholars, appeared conclusive as to the derivation of the Phœnician (and, through that, of all other alphabets now in use) from the Egyptian characters. The success which appeared to attend M. de Rougé's researches "must be attributed to his clear perception of the fact, itself antecedently probable, that the immediate prototypes of the Semitic letters must be sought, not, as had hitherto been vainly attempted, among the hieroglyphic pictures of the Egyptian monuments, but among the cursive characters which the Egyptians had developed out of their hieroglyphs, and which were employed for literary and secular purposes, the hieroglyphic writing being reserved for monumental and sacred uses" (Taylor, i. p. 90). The method which he adopted was admirable. He took the oldest known forms of the Semitic letters that he could discover, and compared these with the oldest known forms of hieratic writing, confining that comparison to the twenty-five letters of the so-called "Egyptian Alphabet." The materials at his command were of the scantiest. On the Egyptian side hieratic papyri of the new Empire (which began about 1587 B.C.) existed in plenty, but the characters in which they are written are comparatively late. Fortunately, however, among the very few examples of the oldest form of hieratic was the Papyrus Prisse (Fig. 50), and this precious relic supplied M. de Rougé with the cursive characters which made formulation of his theory possible. On the Semitic side there are the Egyptian words which are given in Semitic form in the Old Testament, and the Semitic names of Syrian towns which are found in the Egyptian annals of conquests under the new Empire, through which the sounds severally represented by the Semitic and hieratic characters are arrived at. The chief source of epigraphic evidence was an inscription (Fig. 51) on the sarcophagus of Eshmunazar, king of Sidon, dating from the fifth century B.C., or about two thousand years later than the Papyrus Prisse, and therefore representing a late form of the Phœnician alphabet.

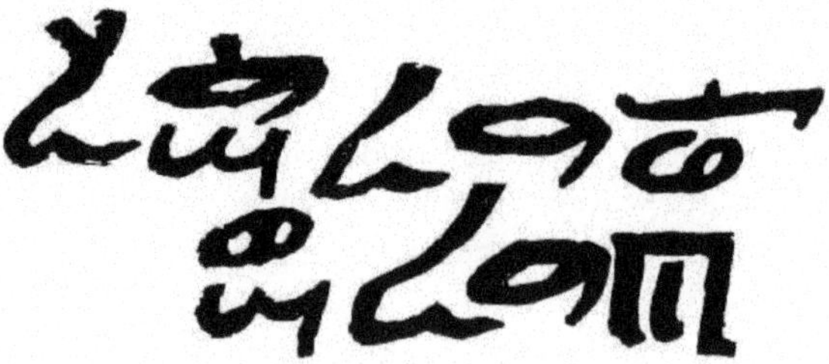

Fig. 50.—Facsimile of Hieratic Papyrus Prisse

The sarcophagus, which is preserved in the Louvre, was found in a rock-tomb near the site of ancient Sidon. The interpretation of the inscription upon it has exercised the skill of a host of scholars, and given rise to an enormous body of literature. Eshmunazar, whose mask and mummy are sculptured on the sarcophagus, speaks in the first person. He calls himself "king of the Sidonians, son of Tabnit," and tells how he and his mother, the priestess of Ashtaroth, had built temples to Baal Sidon, Ashtaroth, and Emun. He beseeches the favour of the gods, and prays that Dora, Joppa, and the fertile corn-lands of Sharon may ever remain part of his kingdom. Well-nigh in the words of Shakespeare's epitaph, he lays a curse upon him who would molest his grave; such an one "shall have no funeral couch with the Rephaim," that haunt the vasty halls of death. "I am cut off before my time; few have been my days, and I am lying in this coffin and in this tomb in the place which I have built. Oh, then, remember this! may no royal race, may no man open my funeral couch, and may they not seek after treasure, for no one has hidden treasures here, nor move the coffin out of my funeral couch, nor molest me in this funeral bed by putting in it another tomb." (Records of the Past, vol. ix.)

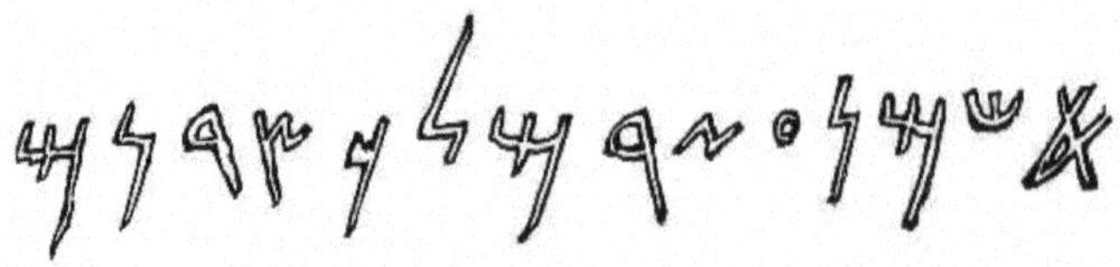

Fig. 51.—Inscription on the Eshmunazar Sarcophagus

Such, broadly speaking, were M. de Rougé's materials for observation and comparison, and there have been few more striking examples of ingenuity of classification and inference than those which, his work supplies. In his excellent summary of that work which Canon Taylor gives in the first volume of his indispensable History of the Alphabet (pp. 98-116), he refers the student who desires full details to M. de Rougé's posthumous Mémoire sur l'origine Égyptienne de l'alphabet Phénicien, and suggests that those readers who care only for results may even skip his summary. That summary necessarily includes much technical matter which will interest only the trained philologist; and in the superficial survey of the subject which is only possible, and perhaps desirable, in these pages, any details would be out of place. Nevertheless, the accompanying tabulated form of M. de Rougé's results may be followed by an example or two of the method which secured them, and also by reference to some earlier Semitic inscriptions which have come to light since 1859.

M. DE ROUGÉ'S THEORY OF THE ORIGIN OF THE ALPHABET.

I. Egyptian Hieroglyphics, facing to the left.

II. Egyptian Hieratic characters, facing to the right.

III. The oldest Phœnician letters, mostly from the Baal Lebanon inscription.

IV. The oldest Greek letters, from inscriptions at Thera and Athens, reading from right to left.

V. The lapidary Greek alphabet at the time of the Persian war, reading from left to right.

VI. Greek uncials, from the Codex Alexandrinus, about 400 A.D.

VII. Greek minuscules.

VIII. The old alphabet of Italy.

IX. Lapidary Latin alphabet at the time of Cicero.

X. Latin uncials and minuscules.

XI. Modern square Hebrew, derived from the Phœnician letters in Col. III.

Our examples of M. de Rougé's method may be taken from the letters b and h.

b. The Egyptians had two signs for this, the "leg,"  which is the normal sign, and the "crane" (see Fig. 2 in foregoing table), which letter should be taken as the prototype of the Phœnician (see Fig. 2, col. iii.). The reason may be that the sound of the first symbol seems to have been nearer to v than to b, the "crane" being used as the equivalent of beth in the translation of several Semitic names, such as Berytus (Beyrout) and Khirba. The hieratic trace of the "leg" would, moreover, be easily confused with that of some other letters, such as the "chick" and the "arm," and would therefore be inconvenient for adoption. The Semitic character 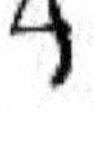 differs from its hieratic prototype  in having acquired a closed loop. The closed form is so much easier to write that the change presents no difficulty. But there is a curious bit of indirect evidence which seems to show that the Semitic in its earlier form was open, something in the shape of an  . The Greek alphabet used at Corinth, one of the earliest Phœnician colonies in Hellas, must have been derived from a type of the Semitic alphabet more archaic than that which appears on the Moabite Stone (see p. 147). Now, in the old Corinthian alphabet the letter beta is not closed, but open,  , its form being almost identical with the hieratic prototype.

h. The letter he corresponds to the "mæander" and the "knotted cord." The hieratic forms show that the former must be taken as the prototype. In the Papyrus Prisse there are two of this character; one, which is comparatively rare, is open at the bottom,  , and corresponds to the Moabite  . It is much more usual, however, to find the character completely closed. The name of the Semitic letter, which is generally supposed to mean a "window," would indicate that the previous form of the letter agreed with the more usual hieratic trace. This conjecture is curiously confirmed by the evidence afforded by the early inscriptions of Corinth, which, as we have seen in the case of beta, occasionally preserve alphabetic forms of a more archaic type than those found on the Moabite Stone itself. Now, in the primitive alphabet of Corinth we find, instead of the usual form of epsilon, a closed character  which is nearly identical with the form of the "mæander," most usual in the Papyrus Prisse. (Taylor, i. pp. 102, 114.)

Among the more important Semitic inscriptions, other than that on the Eshmunazar sarcophagus, are: (1) the inscription on fragments of sacred vessels of bronze from the temple of Baal Lebanon, which is assigned to the eleventh century B.C.; (2) the inscription of Mesha, king of Moab, on a slab of black basalt, known as the Moabite Stone, which is assigned to the ninth century B.C.; (3) the lion weights from Nineveh, bearing the names of Assyrian kings who reigned during the second half of the eighth century B.C.; and (4) the inscription on a tablet in a tunnel which conveys water from the Virgin's Pool in the Kedron Valley to the Pool of Siloam in the Tyropæon. The date of this inscription lies between the eighth and the sixth centuries B.C.

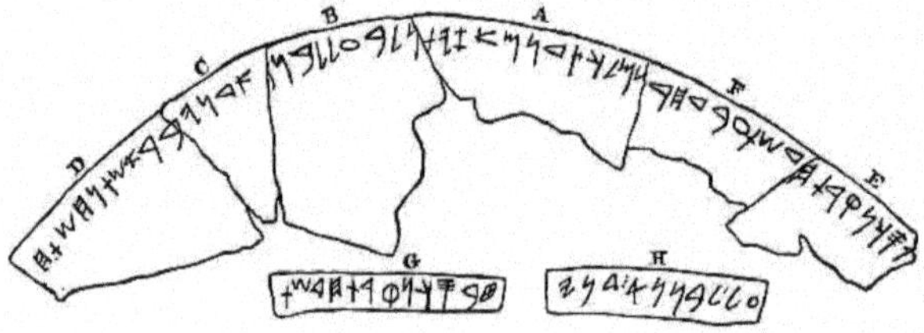

Fig. 52.—Inscription on Sacred Bowls (Baal Lebanon)

1. The Baal Lebanon Vessels. In 1876 M. Clermont-Ganneau bought from a Cypriote dealer some fragments of bronze plates bearing Phœnician characters (Fig. 52). They were traced to a peasant who had found them when digging, and who had broken up the metal in the hope that it was of gold. The industry and skill of MM. Renan and Clermont-Ganneau pieced the fragments together in such wise as to warrant the inference that they were portions of sacred bowls, an inference confirmed by the longest of the inscriptions, which declared that "this vessel of good bronze was offered by a citizen of Carthage, servant of Hiram, king of the Sidonians, to Baal Lebanon, his Lord," whose temple was one of the "high places" dedicated to the god.

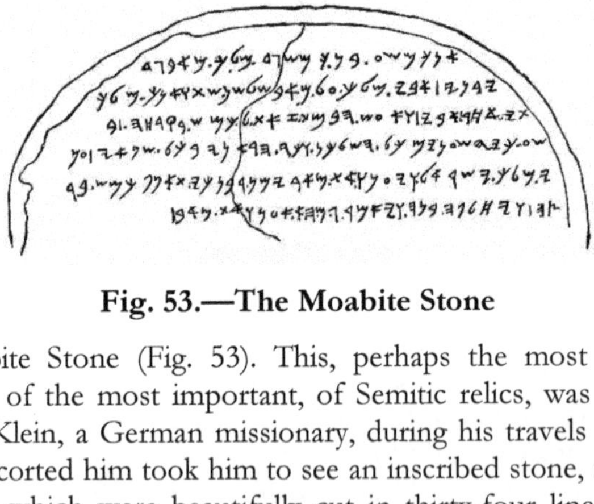

Fig. 53.—The Moabite Stone

2. The Moabite Stone (Fig. 53). This, perhaps the most famous, and, certainly, one of the most important, of Semitic relics, was discovered in 1868 by Dr. Klein, a German missionary, during his travels in Moab. The Arabs who escorted him took him to see an inscribed stone, the Phœnician characters on which were beautifully cut in thirty-four lines. The doctor copied a few words, and resumed his journey. On reaching Jerusalem he made known his discovery, whereupon competition was started between the French and German Consulates for purchase of the coveted treasure. This aroused the suspicion of the Arabs, to whom the stone had become a sort of talisman on which the fertility of their crops depended—that is, when they had industry enough to plant them. Messengers sent by M. Clermont-Ganneau succeeded in taking a squeeze of the inscription, which made the Arabs still more hostile, and in the end, after the Turkish

governor of Nablus had vainly tried to secure the stone for himself—of course to sell at a profit to the "infidel"—the Arabs put a fire under it, then poured cold water over it, and smashed it into fragments, which were distributed as charms among the tribe. But the tact of M. Clermont-Ganneau recovered nearly all the pieces, so that, a few lines excepted, the inscription is complete. The original is preserved in the Louvre, and a very good cast of it may be seen in the Phœnician department of the British Museum.

The inscription, which is written in a language resembling closely the Hebrew of the Old Testament, gives Mesha's account of his rebellion against the King of Israel, to whom he had hitherto paid yearly tribute of the wool of a hundred thousand lambs and a hundred thousand rams. Historically the monument is of high value. Mesha speaks of himself as the son of Chemoshmelek, whose position as the national god of the petty kingdom of Moab corresponds to that of Yahweh or Jehovah among the Israelites. The reference to Chemosh throws light on the correspondences in belief between the several Semitic peoples. The "high place" or altar of the god, his anthropomorphic character as angry, as urging his votaries to battle and to slaughter of their foes, giving them no quarter—all this is identical with the Hebrew conception of deity, so that the inscription, mutatis mutandis, reads like a transcript from the warlike annals of the Old Testament. From the epigraphic standpoint, which alone concerns us here, the inscription is regarded by Canon Taylor and other scholars as supporting the theory of M. de Rougé.

3. The Lion Weights (Fig. 54). Several examples of these were found by the late Sir Austin Layard in his first excavations at Nineveh. They are bilingual, the names of the Assyrian kings being usually in cuneiform writing, while the weights are indicated in Phœnician characters. Of course this evidences intimate trading relations between Assyria and Phœnicia, and the commercial dominance of the latter in the adoption of its weights and measures as the metrical standard of the former, and in the general use of the Phœnician alphabet for business purposes. The action of time has largely obliterated the inscriptions, but among the names of Assyrian kings which have been identified are Tiglath-Peser, Shalmaneser IV., Sargon II., and Sennacherib. The similarity between the Phœnician and Assyrian characters is shown in the inscription here reproduced, which is to scale of the original. It is on the eleventh lion, which weighs a little over twenty ounces, and therefore represents a maneh, a Hebrew weight used in estimating gold and silver, and believed to contain one hundred shekels of the former and sixty of the latter. The reading is MaNeH MeLeK, "a maneh of the king." The name is not very legible, but is read by Professor Sayce as Shalmaneser, who reigned in the seventh century B.C.

Fig. 54.—Maneh Weight

4. The Siloam Inscription.—The tunnel in which this was found was doubtless constructed to secure the water supply of Jerusalem in the event of a siege, the Virgin's Pool being outside the city walls, while the Pool of Siloam is inside the boundaries of the old rampart. Encrustations of carbonate of lime made the decipherment of the letters very difficult on their first discovery in 1880, but enough was seen to prove their high importance for the study of the development of the Hebrew alphabet in its passage from the Phœnician to the Aramean type, whence the modern characters are derived. "It was recognised at once that a Hebrew inscription of a date prior to the Captivity had at last been discovered, and that the uncertainties as to the nature of the alphabet of Israel would now be set at rest." The letters were carefully cleared of their accretion; squeezes, tracings, and casts were obtained, and the Hebrew record, engraved in Phœnician characters nearly resembling those on the Moabite Stone, thus Englished, of course more or less conjecturally in detail, by Professor Sayce:—

(Behold the) excavation! Now this is (1) the history of the tunnel. While the excavators (were lifting up)

the pick each to his neighbour, and while there (2) were yet three cubits (to be broken through) ... the voice of one call-

-ed to his neighbour, for there was (an excess?) in the (3) rock on the right. They rose up ... they struck on the west of the

excavation, the excavators struck each to meet his (4) neighbour pick to pick, and there flowed

the waters from their outlet to the Pool for the (5) distance of 1000 cubits and (three-fourths?)

of a cubit was the height of the rock at the head (6) of the excavation here.

The inscription is interesting if only as showing how modern methods of tunnelling were anticipated by these ancient engineers. One gang of men began boring at one end and another gang at the other end, thus advancing till both met, and the failure to make the connection which is spoken of in "the (excess) in the rock on the right" has confirmation in the existence of two "blind alleys" in the tunnel, showing how the borings overlapped. The accuracy with which, aided by the most recent appliances worked by compressed air, the passages through miles of rock have been bored until the men at either end meet face to face in the middle, is among the romantic achievements of modern science. The Samaritan alphabet is the sole surviving lineal descendant of the Phœnician, which in whatever degree the parent of all extant alphabets, became extinct with the decline of Phœnicia herself, and the characters are now recoverable only through the inscriptions of which examples have been given.

M. de Rougé's theory of the source of that alphabet, and of the variants to which it has given rise, has not passed unchallenged. It belongs to the class of hypotheses which lend themselves to the straining of facts in their support, and therefore demand evidence amounting to demonstration. The superficial resemblances between the written characters are cited as proof of relation, no play being given to that independence of origin of which numerous examples occur in other branches of human development. In his article on Hieroglyphics in the Encyclopædia Britannica, Mr. Reginald Poole remarks that "the hieratic forms vary, like all cursive forms of writing, with the hand of each scribe. Consequently, the writers who desire to establish their identity with Phœnician can scarcely avoid straining the evidence." Moreover, the long lapse of time between the materials for comparison invites caution. The Papyrus Prisse is, at least, two thousand years older than the Eshmunazar inscription, and on these two hang the validity of M. de Rougé's theory. Another contention is that certain Semitic letters represent sounds which are peculiar to that language, and for which no equivalent signs could be adopted from the Egyptian, to which, however, the reply is that in the borrowing of characters it suffices to select those representing similar, although not the same, sounds. The objection that the names of the Semitic letters are not those of the hieroglyphs is met by the principle of acrology (see pp. 86, 104). The question is also asked, Why did not the Phœnicians borrow the hieroglyphic instead of the hieratic characters? Mr. Arthur Evans thinks that in some cases this was done, a few of the letters of the Phœnician alphabet coming direct from the pictorial symbols, as Alpha (Alef = an ox), from the hieroglyph of an ox's head; Zeta (zayin = weapons), from the two-edged axe; Sigma (samech = a post), from the sign of a tree; Omikron (Ain = an eye), from the circle used to represent the eye; Eta and E-psilon (cheth = a fence and He = a window), from signs for a wall or door or window. Canon Taylor, however, argues that the derivation must have been on the lines laid down by M. de Rougé, the Semitic alphabet originating among a colony of aliens of that race settled in Lower Egypt, either as slaves, traders, frontier guards, or conquerors. In any case these intruders would be strangers to the religion and the language of the Egyptians. It would, therefore, be more likely that they should make use of the cursive and easy hieratic, which was ordinarily employed in Egypt for secular and commercial purposes, than that they should adopt the difficult sacred script which was reserved by the Egyptian priesthood for monumental and religious uses. This supposition is confirmed by the singular absence of any hieroglyphic monument which can be assigned to the three dynasties of Semitic rulers known as the Hyksos or Shepherd Kings, who were expelled from Lower Egypt by the Theban Ramesides.

Canon Taylor admits that if, among the objections raised by Professor Lagarde, that based on the want of adequate resemblance between the Semitic letters and the hieratic forms can be sustained, M. de Rougé's theory falls to the ground. The Canon, a staunch, although perfectly candid, supporter of that theory, very properly lays stress on the tendency of things borrowed to partake of the character of the borrower. That they are borrowed at all implies a certain adaptableness in them which permits modification of type, especially when the writing has to be inscribed on another kind of material. The early hieratic writing was traced on papyrus with a soft reed-stump, while the Semitic was cut upon a stone with a chisel, to the loss of flowing lines and curves. "Looking broadly at the two scripts, Hieratic and Moabite, we see in the first place that the Semitic writing is distinguished by greater symmetry and greater simplicity. The letters have become more regular and uniform: more angular, more firm, and more erect; the differences in relative size have diminished; the complicated and difficult characters especially being straightened or curtailed." (History of the Alphabet, i. 125.) Summing up the several objections, of which only the more important have been noted here, Canon Taylor, amending nothing in the recent reprint of his book, remains satisfied as to the soundness of M. de Rougé's theory. "Not only is it on a priori grounds the probable solution, not only does it agree with the ancient tradition, not only does it supply a possible and reasonable explanation of the facts, not only is it confirmed by all sorts of curious coincidences, but no objection has been urged against it to which a sufficient answer cannot be found. If we reject M. de Rougé's explanation of the origin of the alphabet, there is practically no rival theory on which to fall back. There are only three other possible sources, none of which can, at present, be regarded in any higher light than as a mere guess. If the Semitic letters were not derived from Egypt they must have been invented by the Phœnicians, or they must have been developed either out of the Hittite hieroglyphics, or out of one of the cuneiform syllabaries." (Ib., p. 130.) The possible relation of the still undeciphered Hittite hieroglyphs to other scripts will have reference presently, and perhaps Deecke's theory of the derivation of the Phœnician from the Assyrian cuneiform has some measure of truth in it. For cuneiform appears to be essentially a Semitic script, and the Phœnicians in their contact with other Semitic peoples would, it may be assumed, have retained and adapted some, if not all, of the cuneiform characters long before they became familiar with Egyptian hieroglyphic or hieratic. Granting, however, all that the upholders of M. de Rougé's theory may demand, their inference as to the direct connection between the Greek and other alphabets and the Phœnician alphabet is not necessarily to be accepted. On this question of relation new and important light is thrown by recent discoveries, whose significance will be dealt with in the following section.

CHAPTER IX
THE CRETAN AND ALLIED SCRIPTS

When treating of the sources whence civilisation flowed westward centuries before Greece and Rome appear, the historian turns to the valleys of the Nile and the Euphrates. For Egypt and Chaldea have meant so much to us all in our search after the chief influences on man's intellectual and spiritual history, and this with increasing warrant, because the more widely investigation is pushed, the more venerable is the past of both countries found to have been. In the case of Babylon we have seen that the art of writing—that index of culture—had passed the pictographic stage long before eight thousand years ago, while the Egyptian hieroglyphs, which probably came in with the dynasties, and therefore date from the reign of Menes, the first historical king, are some thirteen hundred years later, so far as their use in the Nile Valley is concerned. Hence the Babylonian script carries the palm in point of age. Fortunately the records of both these ancient civilisations are fairly continuous, of Babylonia to the downfall of the empire, and of Egypt to the present time. Assessing the contributions of each to human progress, the verdict appears to be in favour of Babylonia, and "we now know that, high as was the development of Egyptian civilisation in certain directions, it was by no means the fertile mother of other civilisations. All modern writers are agreed that religious cults and national customs are exactly what the Greeks did not borrow from Egypt, any more than the Hebrews borrowed thence their religion, or the Phœnicians their commerce." (Mr. Percy Gardner's New Chapters in Greek History, p. 193.) But if Egypt was no "house of bondage" to Israel, it has been the enslaver of Christendom. It fettered a faith, which had flourished in the freedom of the spirit, with Trinitarianism, Mariolatry, and Monasticism. Out of one or another of its triads emerged the dogma of the Christian Trinity, and in the child Horus, seated in the lap of Isis, we see the profound significance of the words, "Out of Egypt have I called my Son." The obelisk that fronts St. Peter's at Rome symbolises the historical fact that approach to the Christian Church is through the pronaos of the Egyptian temple.

Explorations in Greece and the surrounding archipelago within the last few years have brought to light a third venerable centre of culture. About thirty years ago Dr. Schliemann, digging in prehistoric soil, believed that he had found the palace of Odysseus and the towers of Ilios. "The bones of Agamemnon are a show." The world laughed at him, but, if it takes a more sober view of his discoveries than Schliemann did, it has come to recognise their value and to prosecute his work. The remarkable result of these discoveries is, in the words of Mr. D. G. Hogarth, to show that "man in Hellas was more highly civilised before history than when history begins to record his state; and there existed human society in the Hellenic area, organised and productive, to a period so remote that its origins were more distant from the age of Pericles than that age is from our own. We have probably to deal with a total period of civilisation in the Ægean not much shorter than in the Nile Valley." (Authority and Archæology, p. 230.) The general subject cannot be pursued here, and we have to keep to the narrower track opened up within the past five years in the island of Crete by Mr. Arthur J. Evans. His discoveries there establish (1) the fact of an indigenous culture, and (2) of an active intercourse between Crete and Greece, Egypt, Syria, and other countries centuries before the Phœnicians launched their craft upon the midland sea and trafficked with Cypriote and Cretan, or sailed beyond the Pillars of Hercules. Full accounts of Mr. Evans's important work have for the most part been contributed by him from time to time to the memoirs of learned societies, but no statement in popular form has yet appeared. What now follows will therefore be in large degree an abstract of his paper on "Primitive Pictographs and a Præ-Phœnician Script from Crete and the Peloponnese," published in the Journal of Hellenic Studies, vol. xiv., Part II., 1894, pp.270-372, and reprinted under the title Cretan Pictographs, 1895.

Fig. 55.—Vase with incised Characters (Crete)

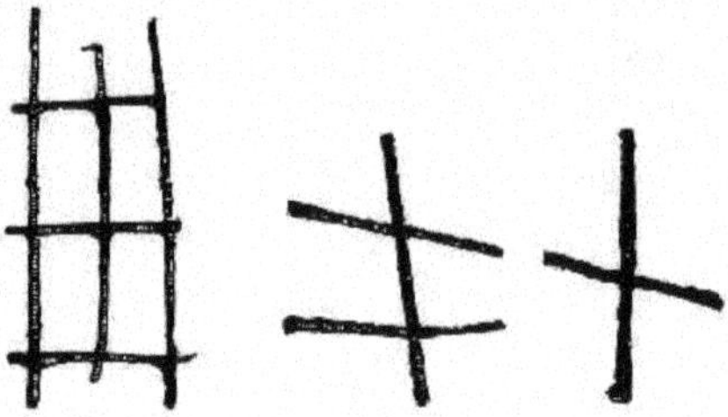

Fig. 56.—Incised Characters on Cup (Crete)

Fig. 57.—Characters on Vase (Crete)

Fig. 58.—Signs on
Bronze Axe (Delphi)

During a visit to Greece in 1893, Mr. Evans came across some small stones bearing engraved symbols which appeared to be hieroglyphic in character, approximating in form to Hittite, but having features of their own. They were traced to a Cretan source, and inquiry in Berlin elicited the fact that the Imperial Museum there possessed stones of corresponding character, which also came from Crete. With this and other corroborative evidence in hand, Mr. Evans decided to follow up his inquiries on Cretan soil, and began his investigations there in the spring of 1894. He chose the eastern part of the island as the more likely district for discovery of prehistoric remains, because, up to the dawn of history, it had been occupied by the "Eteocretes," or primitive non-Hellenic folk. At Praesos he obtained some stones inscribed with hieroglyphic or pictorial, and also with linear, or quasi-alphabetic, characters, the preservation of those objects through the vast lapse of time since they were engraved being largely due to their use as charms by the Cretan women, who wear these "milk-stones," as they call them, during the period of child-bearing. Where, owing to this superstition, Mr. Evans was unable to secure the stones themselves, he obtained impressions of the characters on them. In exploring Goulás, the ruins of which are larger than those of any other prehistoric site, whether in Greece or Italy, Mr. Evans acquired important additions to his collection in the shape (1) of a cornelian gem bearing the image of a rayed sun and a sprig of foliage; (2) of an ox in terra-cotta; and (3) a clay cup on which were three graffito (i.e. rudely scribbled) characters, two of them being identical with the Cypriote pa and lo. A neighbouring hamlet, Prodromos Botzano, yielded a plain terra-cotta vase of primitive aspect with incised hatching round its neck, and three more graffito symbols of the same kind, one of which seemed to represent the double axe-head occurring among the hieroglyphic forms reduced to a linear outline; while the last, as in the clay cup from Goulás, was identical with lo. At another village near Goulás, Mr. Evans procured a double-headed bronze axe with an engraved symbol, with which he compares signs on a bronze axe from Delphi, the first of these looking like a rude outline of a duck or some other aquatic bird. Some of the walls at Knôsos bear certain marks which were at first passed by as mere scratchings by masons, but which Mr. Evans is satisfied are taken from a regular script, and fit on, in fact, to the same system as the characters on the pottery and seals, the various positions in which the signs, as e.g. the double axe, appear, warranting the inference that they were engraved on the blocks before these were placed in situ. Neither these nor the signs graven on the steatite and other small stones are the outcome of mere fancy, or of that cacoêthes scribendi, or "scribbling itch," which wantonly defaces the monuments of past and present times. "Limited as is the number of stones that we have to draw from, it will be found that certain symbols are continually recurring, as certain letters or syllables or words would recur in any form of writing. Thus the human eye appears four times and on as many different stones, the 'broad arrow' seven times, and another uncertain instrument eleven times. The choice of symbols is evidently restricted by some practical consideration, and while some objects are of frequent occurrence, others equally obvious are conspicuous by their absence. But an engraver filling the space on the seals for merely decorative purposes would not thus have been trammelled in his selection." (Jo. Hellenic Studies, p. 300.) Some of the symbols are abbreviated, e.g. the head indicating the whole animal, or a flower the whole plant, thus showing an approach to the ideographic stage of writing. In further example of this there is the expression of ideas and emotions in graphic form, as in the various positions of the arms and hands, and so forth. The symbols also frequently occur in groups of from two to seven, indicating that a syllabic value was given to them, and certain fixed principles of arrangement appear to govern the place of certain signs. Altogether, the conclusion seems warranted that the symbols are not haphazard, but purposive, although, until the materials for judgment have largely increased, the purposes are not easy to particularise. Generally, like all other writing, their object was to tell something, perchance, as already shown (p. 51), information about the avocations of their owners, thus ranking as primitive "merchants' marks."

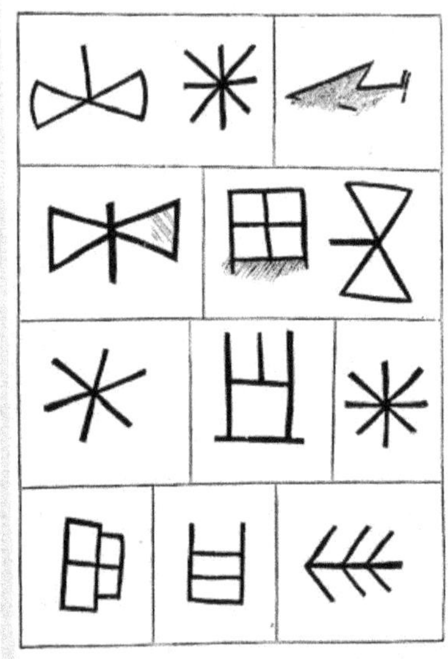

Fig. 59.—Signs on Blocks of Mycenæan Buildings (Knôsos)

Fig. 60.—Symbols on Three-sided Cornelian (Crete)

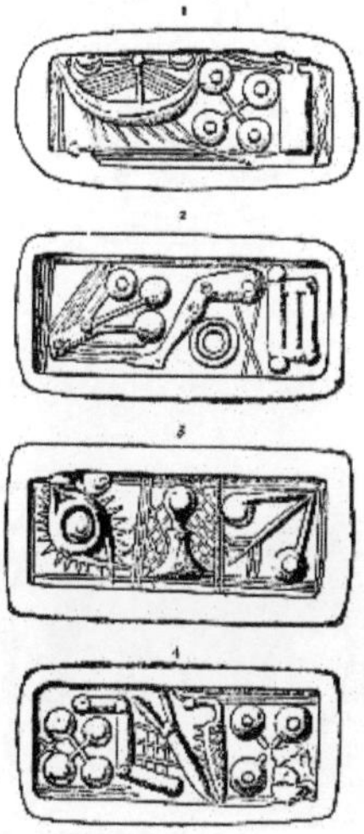

Fig. 61.—Symbols on Four-sided Stone (Crete)

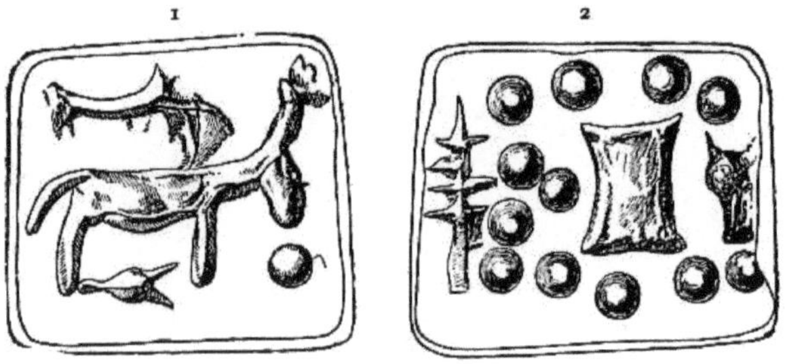

Fig. 62.—Symbols on Four-sided Stones, with larger faces (Central Crete)

Fig. 63.—Symbol on Single-faced Cornelian (Eastern Crete)

Fig. 64.—Symbol on Stone of ordinary Mycenæan type (Athens)

The stones thus bearing symbols of a system of writing in use within the limits of the Mycenæan world in pre-Phœnician times are arranged in five groups by Mr. Evans: (1) three-sided or prism-shaped (Fig. 60); (2) four-sided equilateral (Fig. 61); (3) four-sided with larger faces (Fig. 62); (4) with one engraved side, the upper part being ornamented with a convoluted relief (Fig. 63); (5) stones of ordinary Mycenæan type (Fig. 64).

The HIEROGLYPHIC symbols engraved on the twenty-one stones described and depicted by Mr. Evans number eighty-two, and comprise pictorial and ideographic forms, summarised by him as follows:—

1. The human body and its parts	6
2. Arms, implements, and instruments	17
3. Parts of houses and household utensils	8
4. Marine subjects	3
5. Animals and birds	17
6. Vegetable forms	8
7. Heavenly bodies and derivatives	6
8. Geographical or topographical signs	1
9. Geometrical figures	4
10. Uncertain symbols	12
Total:	82

From the foregoing, all of which are represented in Mr. Evans's monograph, these may be selected as examples:—

1. a. Ideògraph of a man with arms held downwards, perhaps to denote ownership. Human figures in like position, are frequent on Cypriote cylinders.

b. Ideograph of gesture which may indicate ten or any multiple of ten.

2. a. This type of double axe is non-Egyptian. As a Hittite hieroglyph it has been found on an inscription; it is seen repeated in pairs on a Cypriote cylinder, and it also forms the principal type of some Mycenæan gems found at Crete, in the caves of which island bronze axes of this shape are common in the votive deposits.

b. The "arrow" with a short shaft is frequent, one variety showing the feather shaft. Similar figures are occasionally seen in the field of Mycenæan gems found in the island, where they represent arrows of the chase about to strike wild goats or other animals. The Hittite hieroglyphic series presents some close parallels.

1a 1b 2a 2b

3. Gate, door, or part of a fence.

4. a. The first of these vessels is accompanied with two crescents, one on either side of the mask, perhaps a sign of time as applied to the duration of the voyage (see p. 51). One ship has seven oars visible, the other six. In form these vessels show a great resemblance to those which appear as the principal type on a class of Mycenæan lentoid gems.

b. Apparently a tunny-fish. Fish as hieroglyphic symbols are common to Egypt and Chaldæa.

3 4a 4a 4b

5. a. Head of he-goat. This symbol presents a remarkable similarity to the Hittite hieroglyph of the same object  The Egyptian goat's-head sign is of a different character, the neck being given as well as the head, which is beardless. 

b. Bull or ox. The seal on which it occurs is of primitive type.

c. Bird standing. Birds in a somewhat similar position occur among the Hittite symbols at Jerabis and Bulgar Maden, and are frequent in Egyptian hieroglyphics.

5a 5b 5c

6. a. Vegetable forms, similar to those found on Hittite monuments.

b. Floral symbol. The dot above both examples probably represents the head of a stamen or pistil, as of the lily.

6a 6a 6a 6b

7. a. Day-star, or sun, with eight revolving rays.

b. Rays. Star-like symbols occur on Syrian and Asianic seal-stones.

c. This symbol, with its swastika-like offshoots, may be of solar import.

The concentric circles may be compared with the Egyptian , Sun with twelve rays, Sep=times, and with the Chinese hieroglyph for sun with its central dot.

7a 7b 7c

8. Apparently hieroglyphics of mountains and valleys, hence "country" or "land." The Egyptian  men=mountain, is applied in the same way as a determinative for "districts" and "countries." As 

snut=granary, it reappears, with one or two heaps of corn in the middle, in the simple sense of a "plot of ground." The Akkadian symbol, which also

means a plot of ground, exhibits a form  similar to the above.

8

8

"In this connection," says Mr. Evans, "a truly remarkable coincidence is observable between the pictographic symbolism of old Chaldæa and that of the Cretans of the Mycenæan period. The linear form of the Akkadian

Ut-tu  shows a sun above the symbol of the ground with a plant growing out of it. But on specimens of Mycenæan gems observed by me in Eastern Crete are seen symbolic or conventional representations of the plant growing out of the ground." (Jo. Hell. Stud., p. 313.)

The LINEAR signs, although treated separately for purposes of convenience, are regarded by Mr. Evans (see Table I) as fundamentally connected with the hieroglyphic, the one, as in other scripts, overlapping the other. As to this connection, however, some doubt exists. The thirty-two characters which Mr. Evans has detected are increased to thirty-eight by Dr. Tsountas (Mycenæan Age, p. 279), while the materials yielding these results received an important addition through Mr. Evans's discovery, in the spring of 1896, of an inscribed steatite slab, associated with numerous votive objects, in the great cave of Mount Dikta, the fabled birthplace of Zeus. "It consists of a fragment of what may be described as a 'Table of Offerings,' bearing part of what appears to be a dedication of nine letters of probably syllabic values, answering to the same early Cretan script that is seen on the seals, and with two punctuations." (Address of Arthur J. Evans to Section H, Anthropology, of the British Association, 1896; Nature, 1st Oct. 1896, p. 531.)

TABLE I

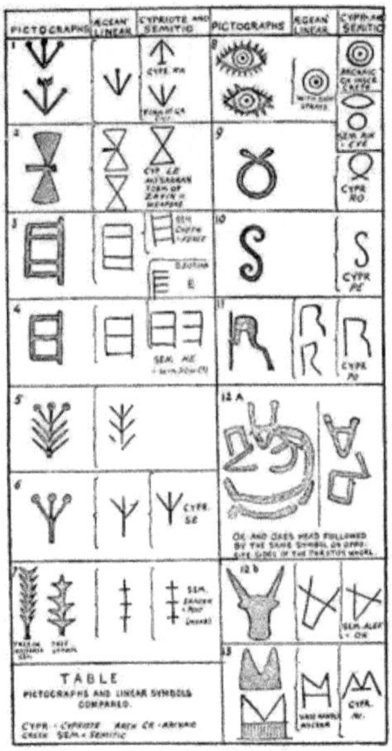

These linear forms are inscribed on three-sided seal stones, in every respect resembling those bearing the pictographic signs; on steatite pendants and whorls; and, as already shown, in graffiti on pottery, or inscribed blocks, and so forth, from all which sources Mr. Evans has put together the thirty-two characters shown in Table II, adding corresponding characters from Cypriote and Egyptian scripts. Table III gives examples of the characters—doubtless syllabic—occurring in groups of two or more.

TABLE II

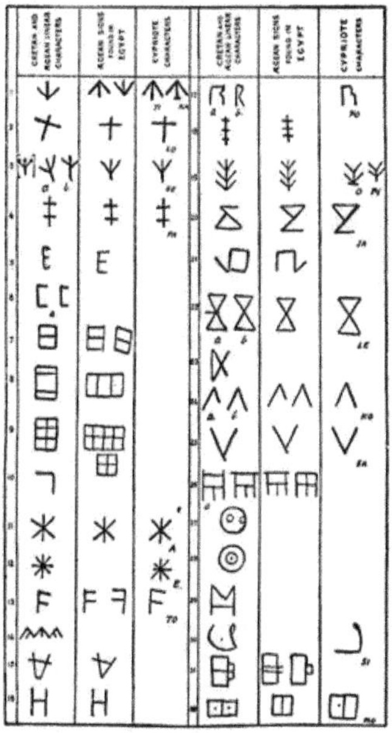

The hieroglyphic-bearing signet stones have been found solely in the region east of Knôsos, and the use of these characters appears not to have passed beyond the island; in fact it may have been limited to the less advanced portions. This tells against the direct descent of the Cretan linear from the Cretan pictographic, and, moreover, it is contended by Dr. Tsountas that the pictographic system exercised slight, if any, influence on the Hellenic portion of Greece. But, in the absence of materials which excavations now being prosecuted may bring to light, any definite conclusions are premature, and only the broadest general views permissible. (The archæological exploration of Crete promises to yield materials of the first importance for knowledge of the history of civilisation in the Eastern Mediterranean area, and the appeal for funds which Mr. Evans and Mr. Hogarth are making should have generous response. Some details of this appeal are printed at the end of this book.) Of the eighty-two pictographic symbols sixteen approach to Egyptian and sixteen to Hittite forms, but all have, none the less, an independent character stamping them as indigenous. Although the coincidences are at times of such a character as to suggest a real affinity, it must be remembered that the similarity in many of the objects to be depicted explains the correspondences between the picture-writing of different peoples. "Some Cretan types present a surprising analogy with the Asianic; on the other hand, many of the most recent of the Hittite symbols are conspicuous by their absence. The parallelism can best be explained by supposing that both systems had grown up in a more or less conterminous

area out of still more primitive pictographic elements. In the early picture-writing of a region geographically continuous there may well have been originally many common elements, such as we find among the American Indians at the present day; and when, later, on the banks of the Orontes and the highlands of Cappadocia on the one side, or on the Ægean shores on the other, a more formalised "hieroglyphic" script began independently to develop itself out of these simpler elements, what more natural than that certain features common to both should survive in each? Later inter-communication may have also contributed to preserve this common element. But the symbolic script with which we have here to deal is essentially in situ. The Cretan system of picture-writing is inseparable from the area dominated by the Mycenæan form of culture. Geographically speaking it belongs to Greece." (Jo. Hellen. Stud., p.317.)

TABLE III

While, as remarked above, the hieroglyph-bearing stones are found only in Crete, examples of the linear character have been found at Mycenæ, Nauplia, and other prehistoric sites in Greece and Egypt. Moreover, as already noted, some of the signs have marked affinities with Cypriote, Hittite, and Semitic.

Among the antiquities which make the Fayum so renowned a district are the remains of two cities; Kahun, which dates from the twelfth dynasty, i.e. 2500 B.C., and Gurob, which is some twelve centuries later, both sites yielding evidence of Asian and Ægean settlers. When digging there ten years ago Professor Flinders Petrie discovered fragments of Mycenæan, or, as he calls it, Ægean, pottery inscribed with characters resembling, and in some cases identical with, those found in Greece. Both the Professor and Mr. Evans agree that the relics unearthed at Kahun are as old as that city; while, speaking of the signs known to be in use 1200 B.C., in a place occupied by people of the Ægean and Asia Minor, Turseni, Akhaians, Hittites, and others, Professor Flinders Petrie remarks that "it will require a very certain proof of the supposed Arabian source of the Phœnician alphabet before we can venture to deny that we have here the origin of the Mediterranean alphabets." (Ten Years' Digging in Egypt, p. 134.) Conversely, scarabs of the twelfth dynasty have been found in Crete, notable among these being one in steatite with a spiral ornament peculiar to that period.

Passing to excavations in the huge mound of Tell-el-Hesy, in Palestine, made up of the ruins of eleven different cities heaped up one above another, we have the discovery, amongst remains of the fourth city, dating about 1450 B.C., of potsherds inscribed with signs similar to the Ægean.

While about twenty per cent. of the Cretan hieroglyphs approach those of the Egyptian in character, twenty out of the thirty-two linear signs there are practically identical with those found in Egypt. Mr. Evans adds that "the parallelism with Cypriote forms is also remarkable, some fifteen agreeing with letters of the Cypriote syllabary."

EGYPTIAN SCARABS, XIITH DYNASTY

EARLY CRETAN SEAL-STONES

Fig. 65.

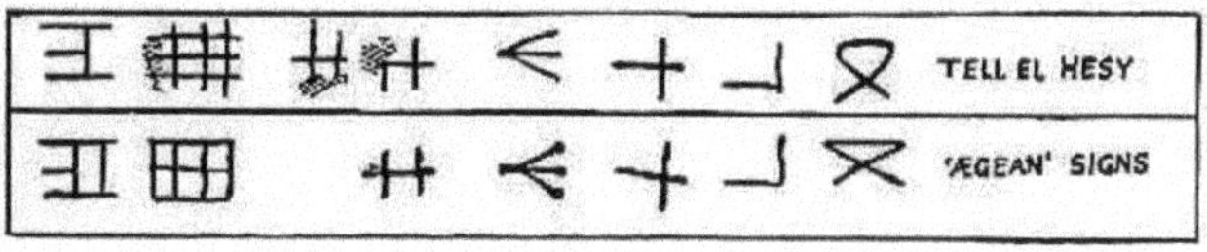

Fig. 65.—Signs on Potsherds at Tell-el-Hesy compared with Ægean Forms

This syllabary, as its name implies, is found in the island of Cyprus,which, lying only sixty miles from Asia Minor, might be expected to yield many traces of active intercourse therewith from prehistoric times. The affinity of its ancient script with those of Western Asia, which may be looked upon as settled, had, therefore, much to commend it at the outset of the inquiry. It stands in nearest relation, possibly as its direct descendant, to the syllabary of the Hittites. References to these people come apace nowadays, and their history has been padded out in portly volumes, but, in truth, we know no more about them than we do about the Phœnicians and Phrygians, which means that we know very little indeed. Through the mists of the past, with the help of such light as is thrown by tablets from Tell-el-Amarna, sculptures from Karnak, and by Hebrew and other records, we have glimpses of a great and powerful empire which stretched from the Euphrates to the Euxine, pushing its borders to the confines of Egypt, against which, on the one hand, and Assyria on the other, it waged war for a thousand years. In 1270 B.C. Rameses III. had to face the onrush of the Hittites and other confederated peoples, whom he defeated at Migdol. They "had overrun Syria. The islands and shores of the Mediterranean gave forth their piratical hordes; the sea was covered with their light galleys, and swept by their strong oars." (Rawlinson's History of Ancient Egypt, vol. ii. p. 271.) According to Dr. Wright, the Hittites appear in history for the first time "in the inscription of Sargon I., King of Agané, about 1900 B.C., and disappear from history in the inscriptions of Sargon 717 B.C." (Empire of the Hittites, p. 122.) Until some thirty years ago no monumental remains had come to light concerning an empire whose high place among ancient nations is attested by the discovery of a treaty (the oldest known example of its kind) with Egypt, in which each recognised the other as a power equal in rank to itself, and agreed to help it in case of need. The first Hittite relic, a block of basalt engraved with strange hieroglyphic signs, was found by the traveller Burckhardt in 1812 at Hamah, on the Orontes, but he could not decipher the characters, and the matter was forgotten till 1870, when the stone was rediscovered, and similar relics brought to light. But to this day the key of interpretation is lacking, and scholars await the unearthing of some bilingual monument which shall do for the Hittite hieroglyphs what the Rosetta Stone did for the Egyptian hieroglyphs and the Behistun rock for cuneiform writing. Till this, and more, is effected, we remain in the realm of conjecture about the mighty nation whose beardless soldiers are depicted with daggers in their belts and double-headed axes in their hands on the sculptures of the Nile Valley. Minimising, however, our knowledge of the Hittites to the uttermost, their widely distributed relics evidence their proficiency in certain departments of the arts. They smelted silver and wrought in bronze, they were skilful lapidaries and carvers in ivory, and "the independent system of picture-writing which they possessed offers an obvious source from which the Asianic syllabary might have been obtained." In the Hamah inscriptions the characters are raised, and run in parallel transverse lines.

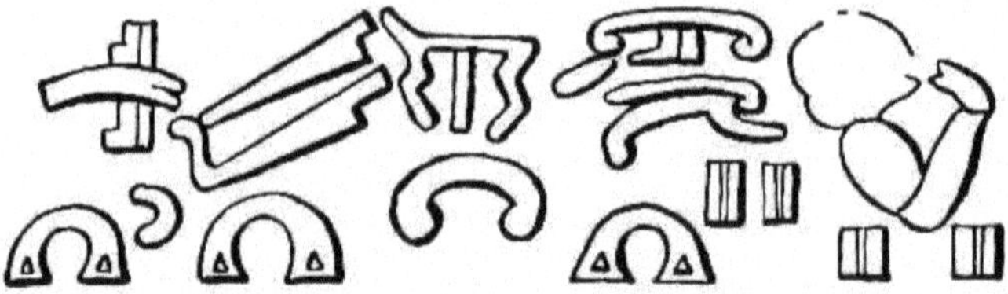

Fig. 67.—Hittite Inscription at Hamah.

"The lines of inscriptions and their boundaries are clearly defined by raised bars about four inches apart. The interstices between the bars and characters have been cut away." The inscriptions are read from right to left and vice versâ in "boustrophedon" style (bous, "an ox," and strephō, "to turn," therefore, as an ox ploughs), as in ancient Greek modes of writing.

Returning to Crete, we have to consider its relation to the Mycenæan type of civilisation, under which term is included civilisation in pre-Homeric Greece and the Ægean Sea, crossing thence to Hissarlik, the ancient Troy. The spade has made havoc with some of our standard "authorities." Grote refers to the city of Mycenæ only once in his well-known work, and then incidentally speaks of it as the seat of a legendary dynasty. Sir George Cox, in his Mythology of the Aryan Nations, endorses Professor Max Müller's theory (to which, in part, the veteran philologist still adheres), that the siege of Troy "is a reflection of the daily siege of the East by the solar powers that every evening are robbed of their brightest treasures in the West," and adds that this theory is "supported by a mass of evidence which probably hereafter will be thought ludicrously excessive in amount." The laugh is on the other side now. Schliemann and his successors have broken into the areas within Cyclopean walls whose massive blocks aroused wonder long ages back, giving birth to tales of giant hands that reared them. They have disinterred relics proving an historic element in old traditions, and a nucleus of fact beneath the encrustation of fable over famous names. Like the Empress Helena, who, in searching for the True Cross, of course found that for which she looked, Schliemann too readily assumed that he had discovered the bones of Agamemnon, and the cup from which Nestor drank. But he brought to light the relics of a culture, knowledge of which involves neither more nor less than the re-writing of the history of man in the Eastern Mediterranean, and, by consequence, in Western Europe.

Fig. 68.—Signs on Vase-handle (Mycenæ)

Fig. 69.—Signs on Amphora-handle (Mycenæ)

Dealing, as the limits of the subject compel, only with the traces of inscriptions on remains from Mycenæ itself, the earliest to be noted is a stone pestle with one incised character which resembles a Cypriote sign. But one sign does not make an alphabet, and hence the satisfaction at the recent discovery of the handle of a stone vase, apparently of a local material, which has four or five signs engraved upon it, and of the handle of a clay amphora from a chambered tomb in the lower town of Mycenæ with three characters, while a tomb at Prousia, near Nauplia, yielded a genuine Mycenæan vessel with three ears, on each of which is graven a sign resembling the Greek H. These may not suffice to demonstrate the existence of a pre-Phœnician system of writing in Greece, but, taken in conjunction with the numerous discoveries of inscribed signs in Crete, they go far in support of it. What, then, are the facts as thus far, ascertained?

There have been discovered in Crete a number of objects bearing two sorts of writing, one hieroglyphic or pictographic; the other linear and approaching the alphabetic. The pictographic is the older of the two, dating from the earlier part of the third millennium before Christ. It was probably derived from a primitive picture-writing by the non-Hellenic inhabitants of the island, who were called Eteocretans, or "true Cretans," by the Dorians, whose invasion dates, according to the traditional Greek chronology, from about the middle of the twelfth century B.C. These "true Cretans" may not, however, be the aboriginal inhabitants, although as to this, and as to their language, we are in ignorance. The recent discovery of an inscription in an unknown language, written in archaic Greek characters, among the ruins of Præsos, the chief Eteocretan settlement, warrants the inference that the old script of the language had been abandoned for the Greek alphabet. That script, the use of which never passed outside the island, obviously had no influence on Mycenæan civilisation.

The linear system is syllabic; perhaps, in some degree, alphabetic. Its possible derivation from the hieroglyphic has been indicated, but although it is a conventionalised form of pictograph, Dr. Tsountas is positive in denying its connection with the Eteocretan. He suggests that its simplification took place in the East, and among a people or peoples not Greek. Thence it was carried into Greek lands, spreading more in the islands, at least in Crete, than in the Peloponnesus or other portions of the mainland, where, as shown above, the number of inscribed objects is exceedingly small. The question is far from ripe for solution, but Professor Flinders Petrie, with whom lies a large share of honour in contributing towards a settlement, courteously permits me to quote the following from a letter on the subject, dated 2nd September 1899: "A great signary (not hieroglyphic, but geometric in appearance, if not in origin) was in use all over the Mediterranean 5000 B.C. It is actually found in Egypt at that period, and was split in two, Western and Eastern, by the cross flux of hieroglyphic systems in Egypt and among the Hittites. This linear signary was developed variously, but retained much in common in different countries. It was first systematised by the numerical values assigned to it by Phœnician traders, who carried it into Greece, whereby the Greek signary was delimited into an alphabet. But the fuller form of the signary survived in Karia with thirty-six signs, and seven more in Iberia, thus giving values to forty-three. This connection of the Iberian with the Karian is striking; so is that of the Egyptian with the West rather than with the East. Signs found in Egypt have thirteen in common with the early Arabian, fifteen in common with Phœnician, and thirty-three in common with Karian and Kelt-Iberian. This stamps the Egyptian signary of the twelfth and eighteenth dynasties as closely linked with the other Mediterranean systems." In an important paper read at the meeting of the British Association, 1899, Professor Flinders Petrie remarks: "We stand therefore now in an entirely new position as to the sources of the alphabet, and we see them to be about thrice as old as had been supposed. That the signs were used for written communications of spelled-out words in the early stages, or as an alphabet, is far from probable. It was a body of signs, with more or less generally understood meanings; and the change of attributing a single letter value to each, and only using signs for sounds to be built into words, is apparently a relatively late outcome of the systematising due to Phœnician commerce." (Jo. Anthrop. Inst., Aug.-Nov., 1899, p. 205.)

Connecting the results of explorations in Asia Minor, Egypt, Crete, Cyprus, Rhodes, Thera, Melos, and other islands of the Eastern Mediterranean with those in the Peloponnesus, the existence of a pre-Phœnician civilisation, of which Mycenæ may be conveniently regarded as the centre, appears to be demonstrated.

That civilisation, so far as its connection with the prehistoric stages of man's development goes, falls in, like aught else in this wide and ancient world, with the doctrine of continuity, but for purposes of time-reckoning dates at latest far back in the third millennium before our era. Mycenæan vases have been found in Egypt, and Egyptian scarabs in Mycenæan deposits. They prove an intimate intercourse between the two countries two thousand five hundred years before Christ. And there was intercourse farther afield. The imitations of Babylonian cylinders, the sculptured palms and lions, the figures of Astarte and her doves, show that fifteen hundred years before the date ascribed to the Homeric poems Assyria and Greece had come into contact. But the examples of Oriental art which had found their way to the soil of Argolis remained more or less exotic, the independent features of Mycenæan art being retained unaltered. Now the cumulative effect of this evidence, which is only baldly summarised here, is to shatter to pieces current theories as to the Phœnician origin of European civilisation, and, consequently, what mainly concerns us here, of the Phœnician origin of the European alphabets through the Egyptian hieratic. For that evidence shows that the Mycenæan civilisation is (1) earlier in time, and (2) indigenous in character.

(1) The evidence as to priority can be summarily stated. Civilisation in the Ægean and on the Greek mainland dates from beyond 3000, B.C., and reached its meridian between the sixteenth and the twelfth centuries of that era. Almost all that we know about the Phœnicians is at second-hand, since, if they ever had a literature or native chronicles, these have not survived. Piecing together classical tradition and references in Egyptian and Hebrew records, we gather that for some three centuries onwards from 1600 B.C. Phœnicia was a dependency of the Pharaohs. There was a Tyrian quarter at Memphis 1250 B.C. Hiram appears to have refounded Tyre 1028 B.C., from which time its commercial importance dates; while the refounding of its future great rival Carthage is assigned to the early years of the eighth century B.C. The decay of the Mycenæan civilisation, which followed as one of the many results of the Dorian invasion in the twelfth century B.C., gave the Phœnicians their chance. They overran the Ægean, and remained the dominant power in the Mediterranean until the Greeks, reviving their ancient traditions, expelled the Phœnicians from their waters, and broke

their supremacy when Tyre was sacked by Alexander the Great, 332 B.C. Between their rise and fall, their commercial pre-eminence enabled them to impose upon the Greeks the alphabet which was the vehicle of preservation of the intellectual wealth of the Hellenes, and of all literature that followed theirs. What were the probable sources of that alphabet will be considered presently.

(2) After allowing full play for Asian and Egyptian influences, the fact abides that there was a well-developed native Mycenæan art. The decoration of the pottery is non-Oriental and non-Egyptian; the seaweeds and marine creatures depicted are home-products of the island world of Greece; and where sacred trees and pillars appear, we have no Semitic element, but the outcome, as Mr. Evans puts it, of a "religious stage widely represented on primitive European soil, and nowhere more persistent than in the West." But if there were stepping-stones between Argolis and Syria in the islands that lay between, there was continuous passage on the western side, making Mycenæ a link between East and West. The breaks formerly assumed between the Old and the New Stone Ages of prehistoric Europe have been filled up by the accumulation of evidence as to man's continuous tenure of that continent since his primitive ancestors crossed thither by now vanished land-routes from Northern Africa. In like manner the Mirage Orientale, as M. Salomon Reinach happily terms it, of a metal-introducing people from the East, who, in successive racial waves, swept the older settlers before them into the remotest corners of the north-west, has vanished. When once peopled, Europe, like Asia and America, ran on independent lines of development, which, however, were not isolated from connecting lines approaching from the East. The striking facts of the use of common trade-signs along both shores of the Mediterranean, and of the existence of remains of Mycenæan monuments in Sardinia, are in keeping with other facts, showing how close was the contact between one part of Europe and another centuries before the Phœnicians had left the shores of the Persian Gulf for the Syrian seaboard. They prepare us for acceptance of the new theory of "an Ægean culture rising in the midst of a vast province extending from Switzerland and Northern Italy through the Danubian basin and the Balkan peninsula, and continued through a large part of Anatolia, till it finally reaches Cyprus." (Evans, Address Brit. Assoc.; Nature, 1st Oct. 1896, p. 529.) They prepare us for the fact that in the Bronze Age, if Scandinavia and its borderlands were the source of amber, the supply of gold for Northern and Central Europe was drawn not from the Ural, but from Ireland.

The centre whence this "Ægean" culture is held to have been diffused is denoted by its name. That name, however, covers the Eastern Mediterranean region, and the question arises whether or not some precise place in that area can be indicated as the cradleland. "Hellas," says Herodotus, "was formerly called Pelasgix" (ii. 56), and this pre-Hellenic Greece was inhabited by Barbarians or Pelasgians, as they are, with equal vagueness, called. There were "Pelasgians" on the mainland and the islands; "the whole of Peloponnesus took the name of Pelasgia; the kings of Tiryns were Pelasgians, and Æschylus calls Argos a Pelasgian city; Pausanias (viii. 4, 6) says that the Arcadians spoke of Pelasgus as the first man who lived in that country, wherefore, in his reign, it was called Pelasgia; an old wall at Athens was attributed to the Pelasgians, and the people of Attica had from all time been so called. Lesbos also was called Pelasgia, and Homer knew of Pelasgians in the Troad. Their settlements are further traced to Egypt, to Rhodes, Cyprus, Epirus—where Dodona was their ancient shrine—and, lastly, to various parts of Italy." (Keane's Man Past and Present, p. 505.) Herodotus has little to say in favour of the Barbarians (which he uses as a descriptive and not a contemptuous term, the name being given by Greeks to all foreigners whose language was not Greek); he speaks of them as rude, of uncouth speech, and worshippers of repellent deities. Wachsmuth, in his Historical Antiquities of the Greeks, published over sixty years ago, says that "numerous traditionary accounts, of undoubted authenticity, describe them as a brave, moral, and honourable people, which was less a distinct stock and tribe than a race united by a resemblance in manners and the forms of life." Professor Keane fitly calls these "remarkable words," in view of the recent discoveries in prehistoric Greece, which warrant us in ascribing to the Pelasgians the development of culture in the Ægean Sea. But in what island, or on what part of the mainland? The important character of the finds at Mycenæ directs quest thither at the start. The débris of that city, and of her elder-sister city, Tiryns, have yielded varied relics of an ancient culture, from gold-masked skeletons in vaulted tombs to gorgeously decorated palaces and Cyclopean ruins of walls and fortresses. But there are traditions that these Argolic cities are of later date than Homer's "great city of Knossos" in Crete, wherein "Minos, when he was nine years old, began to rule, he who held converse with the great Zeus, and was the father of my father, even of Deucalion, high of heart," traditions pointing to the existence of an important Cretan kingdom which flourished before Agamemnon ruled in Mycenæ.

Water is the birthplace of civilisation, as of life itself, and the original home of the Ægean or Mycenæan civilisation is probably to be found in the island of Crete. It is crammed with remains of pre-Hellenic culture. It is a big stepping-stone from Greece to Asia Minor, Karpathos and Rhodes lying between. It is in the line of communication with Cyprus, Syria, and Egypt on the East, and with Sicily and the coastlines of the Western Mediterranean. The earliest Greek tradition looks back to Crete "as the home of divinely inspired legislation and the first centre of maritime dominion." And, what is of the highest moment to remember, so far as the origin of the art of navigation in Ægean waters goes, there can be no question between the old claims on behalf of the Phœnicians and the present claims on behalf of Crete. The Syrian seaboard is harbourless and unsheltered; the men who first braved the "unvintaged wine dark" waters (how fine are all the Homeric sea-words) were island-dwellers, shooting forth from snug creek and harbour on quick and sudden enterprise, and growing bolder and bolder as they sailed by the rising and setting of the stars and the recurring moon. "The early sea-trade of the inhabitants of the island world of the Ægean gave them a start over their neighbours, and produced a higher form of culture, which was destined to react on that of a vast European zone, nay, even upon that of the older civilisations of Egypt and Asia." (Evans, Address, B. Assoc., p. 530.) For the diffusion of culture throughout the Ægean was followed by expeditions to the East. While Cyprus yielded the metal to which it has given its name, the gold of Asia Minor was poured into the lap of the pre-Hellenes, and moulded into forms of beauty through which their own artistic skill challenged comparison with that of the Oriental. In his comment on the source of the Mycenæan civilisation Mr. Frazer aptly remarks that "the existence at this early date of a great maritime power in Crete, which by its central position between Greece and the empires of the East was well fitted to receive and amalgamate the characteristics of both, is just what is needed to explain the rise and wide diffusion of a type of civilisation like the Mycenæan, in which Oriental influences seem to be assimilated and transmuted by a vigorous and independent nationality endowed with a keen sense of its own for art. The spade will probably one day decide the question of priority between Argolis and Crete, but in the meantime the probability appears to be that the Mycenæan civilisation rose in Crete and spread from it as a centre, and that it was not until the Cretan power was on the wane that the palmy days of Tiryns and Mycenæ began." (Commentary on Pausanias, vol. iii. p. 151.) The Mycenæan civilisation perished in a great catastrophe. Somewhere near the middle of the twelfth century B.C. the Dorian invaders in their southward march reached the walls of Tiryns and Mycenæ, and sacked and gave those cities to the flames. Then began for Greece "the long dark ages, the mediæval epoch, out of which she emerges only in the Homeric Renaissance." The flower of the survivors of that dread time sought a new home east of the Ægean on the isles and shores of Ionia. There these exiles from Argolis laid the foundation of a culture whose influence will abide while the world stands, because Ionia remains the fatherland of all who hold dear what man has reached in art and literature, in science and philosophy.

The fall of Mycenæ gave Phœnicia her opportunity, and she was quick to seize it in establishing depôts throughout the Ægean, and in securing the overlordship of the Mediterranean. But through her lack of political unity, and her dependence on mercenary aid when troubles came, finally she succumbed to the strong arm of the reinvigorated Greek. Between their rise and decline the Phœnicians had put the alphabet into, practically, its present form, and secured its adoption by the Greeks. But if they did not derive it from the Egyptian hieratic, whence came it?

No definite answer is forthcoming, and perhaps never will be. Canon Rawlinson is not alone in thinking that it will probably never be settled whether the Phœnician characters are modifications of the Egyptian or the Hittite or of Cypriote, or mere abbreviated forms of a picture-writing peculiar to the Phœnicians. That opinion was expressed before the discovery of the Cretan pictographs and linear signs, and these have not settled the question. The Phœnicians came under various influences, and their adaptive character readily took the impress of their surroundings. Probably they had a long history before they appear in Syria. As Semites, they were presumably familiar with cuneiform. The Tyrian quarter at Memphis was one of many settlements where the Egyptian characters would be in use, or, at least, familiar. And when the Phœnicians came into the Ægean they found an ancient script whereby intercourse was facilitated along the Mediterranean, a script of which so pliant a people, eager for trade, would avail themselves. In view of all these probabilities, Mr. Evans remarks that it is at least worth while weighing "the possibility that the rudiments of the Phœnician writing may after all have come in part at least from the Ægean side. The more the relics of Mycenæan culture are revealed to us, the more we see how far ahead of their neighbours on the Canaanite coasts was the Ægean population in arts and civilisation." The spread of their commerce led them to seek plantations in the Nile Valley and the Mediterranean outlets of the Arabian and Red Sea trade. The position was the reverse of that which meets our eye at a later date. It was not Sidon that was then planting mercantile settlements on the coasts and islands of Greece." (Jo. Hellen. Stud., p. 368.) Whether, per contra, a Semitic element had been introduced into the Ægean is uncertain, but could this be proved, the presence of similarities between the respective scripts would have easy explanation. Putting together, however, what is no longer conjectural, it would seem that the Phœnician alphabet was a compound from various sources, the selection and modification of the several characters being ruled by convenience, and that, primarily and essentially, commercial. Like all business people immersed in many transactions, their method was brevity, and so they aimed as near "shorthand" as they could. They got rid of surplus signs, of the lumber of determinatives and the like, and invented an alphabet which if it was not perfect (as no alphabet can be, because the letters are not revised from time to time to represent changes in sound), was of such signal value as to have been accepted by the civilised world of the past, and to have secured, with but slight modifications, a permanence assured to no other invention of the human race. Therefore, the debt that we owe these old traders is in nowise lessened because the current theory of derivation of our alphabet is doubted. This theory as to the nature of the service rendered by the Phœnicians has corroboration in an ancient Cretan tradition recorded by Diodôros, a contemporary of Julius Cæsar and Augustus, to which Mr. Evans makes reference in the reprint of his essay. According to that tradition, the Phœnicians had not invented written characters, but had simply "changed their shapes." In other words, they had not done more than improve on an existing system, which is precisely what recent evidence goes to show. "We may infer from the Cretan contention recorded by Diodôros that the Cretans claimed to have been in possession of a system of writing before the introduction of the Phœnician alphabet. The present discovery on Cretan soil both of a pictographic and a linear script dating from times anterior to any known Phœnician contact thus affords an interesting corroboration of this little regarded record of an ancient writer." (Cretan Pictographs, p. 372.)

CHAPTER X
GREEK PAPYRI

The Greeks succeeded to the sovereignty of the sea after they had driven the Phœnicians from the Ægean. They were skilful shipbuilders and navigators, and their maritime enterprise, in which, as has been shown, they preceded the Phœnicians, took a new lease of life from the eighth century B.C. Their factories and colonies were planted from east to west, from Odessa to Marseilles, where, as their farthermost point, we find them settled 600 B.C. The assistance given by Ionians and Carians to Psammetichus, the first king of the twenty-sixth dynasty (666 B.C.) in his war with the Assyrians was rewarded by the assignment of permanent settlements in Egypt, and in the reign of his son, Necho II., the cities of Sais and Naucratis (about both of which Herodotus has much to say, ii. 97, 135, 169, 178, &c.) was full of Greek colonists, to whose commercial and intellectual activity the then prosperous state of Egypt was mainly due. The footing which they obtained there was secured when, three hundred years later, Alexander the Great marked his conquest in the founding of the city which bears his name. It is well to keep these facts in mind, because in our assessment of the debt of the civilised world to Greece we are apt to forget that it was not wholly intellectual, but also social and industrial. And these facts have bearing on our immediate subject in explaining the spread of the Greek alphabet, or, more precisely, the Western or Chalcidian form of it, whence the Latin, and through it the alphabets of Europe and America, are derived. Although the name was limited to the districts in the south of Italy, in the larger sense of the term Græcia Major corresponds to Greater Britain. As with the area of our home islands compared with that of our colonies, so was it with Hellas and her expansion along the sea whose waters laved the coasts of the civilised world. And the spread of the English language and the English alphabet over half the civilised globe may be compared with "the diffusion of Hellenic culture and Hellenic scripts throughout the Mediterranean region, originating in the pre-Christian centuries various derived alphabets—Iberian, Gaulish, Etruscan, Latin, and Runic, followed at a later time by the Mæso-Gothic, Albanian, &c." (Taylor, ii. 125.)

Palæography, or the decipherment of documents, and Epigraphy, or the decipherment of inscriptions, have been indispensable keys to the history of the alphabet. But the materials with which each has to deal would demand a volume, and, moreover, reference to them here has warrant only in their immediate bearings on the development and diffusion of alphabets.

But, as with the Papyrus Prisse and the Book of the Dead, there is a deep interest attaching to some of the venerable records. They are, in the modern phrase, and in the best sense of it, "human documents." Such are the Greek papyri, the oldest-known specimens of which are found in Egypt, and have a range of a thousand years, i.e. from the third century B.C. to the seventh century A.D., so that, as Mr. Kenyon remarks in his monograph on the subject, "we may fairly say that we know how men wrote in the days of Aristotle and Menander, but we have not yet got back to Pindar and Æschylus, much less to Homer or (if a less contentious name be preferred) Hesiod." The use of papyrus as a writing material stretches back in Egypt to a remote antiquity; but we cannot be certain that it was used by the Greeks before the early part of the fifth century B.C., while "with the Arab conquest of Egypt (640 A.D.) the practice of Greek writing on papyrus received its death-blow." By far the larger number of documents thus far discovered are non-literary, dealing with official and commercial matters, as tax-collectors' receipts (although many of these are scratched on potsherds, or ostraca, literally "oyster shells," whence ostracize, the inscribing of the name of a person obnoxious to the state on a shell), acknowledgments of repayment of dowry after divorce, wills, reports of public physicians on autopsy, house-keeping bills, surety deeds, registration of title to inheritance, wedding and dinner invitations, of which last here is an example eighteen hundred years old: "Chæron requests your company at dinner at the table of Lord Serapis in the Serapæum to-morrow, the 15th, at 9 o'clock" (i.e. about 3 P.M.). Then there are domestic letters, one, touching human hearts across the centuries, from a father to his son: "Tell me anything I can do for you. Good-bye, my boy;" and another crudely written, and with faulty spelling and grammar, from a boy to his father. "Theon to his father Theon, greeting: It was a fine thing of you not to take me with you to Alexandria. I won't write a letter or speak to you, or say good-bye to you, and if you go to Alexandria I won't take your hand, nor ever greet you again. That is what will happen if you won't take me.... Send me a lyre, I implore you; if you don't, I won't eat, I won't drink. There, now!"

The first discovery of Greek papyri was made at Herculaneum in 1752. They consist of above eighteen hundred charred rolls, which were enclosed in a wooden cabinet, and doubtless formed a portion of the library of one Lucius Piso Cæsonius, in the ruins of whose villa they were found. The condition of the papyri made the unrolling and decipherment of them a very tedious operation, and the work is not even yet completed. "They are written in small uncial letters, and possess little beyond palæographic value, comprising worthless treatises on physics, music, rhetoric, and kindred subjects by Philodemus and other third-rate philosophers of the Epicurean school." A quarter of a century later some rolls of papyrus were found in

Egypt, probably in the Fayum. Of these only one, containing a list of peasants employed in the corvée, survived destruction by the natives, and it was not till 1820 that the discovery of a number of rolls on the site of the Serapeum at Memphis supplied the key to knowledge of Greek writing of the second century B.C. Since then, at varying intervals, the finds have increased in number and importance. The earliest known examples, dating from the third century B.C., were discovered by Professor Flinders Petrie in 1889 in a number of mummy cases at Gurob. Most of these papyri were non-literary—wills, petitions, and such-like documents—but two valuable relics came to light in fragments of Plato's Phædo and the lost Antiope of Euripides. Then followed the discovery of another lost work, Aristotle's **Αθηναίων Πολιτεία**; of the Mimes of Herodas—an almost unknown writer of the Alexandrian age—part of another oration of Hyperides; a long medical treatise, and fragments of Homer, Demosthenes, and Isocrates. The Mimes, two thousand years old, are as young as yesterday. "Though," Mr. Whibley remarks in a charming paper upon these recovered treasures, "they have survived the searching test of time, they have been unseen of mortal eyes for countless centuries. The emotions which Herodas delineates are not Greek, but human, and no preliminary cramming in archæology is necessary for their appreciation. As the world was never young, so it will never grow old. The archæologist devotes years of research to compiling a picture of Greek life, and the result is Charicles—a cold and unrelieved mass of 'local colour.' There is no proportion, no atmosphere, no background; all is false save the details, and they merely overload the canvas. Herodas presents not a picture, but an impression, and one mime reveals more of life as it was lived two thousand years ago, than the complete works of Becker, Ebers, and the archæologists." (Nineteenth Century, Nov. 1891, p. 748.) Here is one scene by which Mr. Whibley justifies his appreciation. The dramatis personæ are Metriche, a grass-widow; Threissa, her maid; and Gyllis, an old lady.

Metriche. Threissa, there is a knock at the door; go and see if it is a visitor from the country.

Threissa. Please push the door. Who are you that are afraid to come in?

Gyllis. All right, you see, I am coming in.

Threissa. What name shall I say?

Gyllis. Gyllis, the mother of Philainis. Go indoors, and announce me to Metriche.

Threissa. A caller, ma'am.

Metriche. What, Gyllis, dear old Gyllis! Turn the chair round a little, girl. What fate induced you to come and see me, Gyllis? An angel's visit, indeed!

Why, I believe it's five months since any one dreamt of your knocking at my door.

Gyllis. I live such a long way off, and the mud in the lane is up to your knees. I am ever anxious to come, for old age is heavy upon me, and the shadow of death is at my side.

Metriche. Cheer up! don't malign Father Time; old age is wont to lay his hand on others too.

Gyllis. Joke away; though young women can find something better to do than that. But, my dear girl, what a long time you've been a widow. It's ten months since Mandris was despatched to Egypt, and he hasn't sent you a single line; doubtless he has forgotten you, and is drinking at a new spring; for in Egypt you may find all things that are or ever were—wealth, athletics, power, fine weather, glory, goddesses, philosophers, gold, handsome youths, the shrine of the god and goddess, the most excellent king, the finest museum in the world, wine, all the good things you can desire, and women, by Persephone, countless as the stones and beautiful as the goddesses that appealed to Paris.

Metriche protests, and Gyllis, suggesting that Mandris is dead, reveals the purpose of her visit.

Now listen to the news I have brought you after this long time. You know Gyllus, the son of Matachene, who was such a famous athlete at school, got a couple of blues at his university, and is now amateur champion bruiser? Then he is so rich, and he leads the quietest life; see, here is his signet-ring. Well, he saw you the other day in the street, and was smitten to the heart. And, my dear girl, he never leaves my house day or night, but bemoans his fate, and calls upon your name; he is positively dying of love.

Metriche becomes righteously indignant when Gyllis suggests that she return this love.

By the fates, Gyllis, your white hairs blunt your reason. There is no cause yet to deplore the fate of Mandris. By Demeter, I shouldn't like to have heard this from another woman's lips. And you, my dear, never come to my house with such proposals again. For none may make mock of Mandris.... But, if what the world says be true, I needn't speak to Gyllis like this. Threissa, let us have some refreshments; bring the decanter and some water, and give the lady something to drink. Now, Gyllis, drink, and show that you aren't angry.

And so with delightful interchange of civilities the quarrel is brought to an end.

Passing by other discoveries, some of these including fragments of a play by Menander, of whose hundred comedies none are perfect, we come to the thousands of Greek papyri found in 1896-97 by Messrs. Grenfell and Hunt on the site of the ancient Oxyrhynchus, the capital of a nome of Middle Egypt. The full list of these relics has not yet been published, and it will take some years to decipher them all; but among the literary portion are fragments of works known and unknown. Among the latter is a papyrus of the second century, containing a collection of Logia, or Sayings, of Jesus Christ, some of which are familiar, whilst others are wholly new. The following translation of these, made by the Rev. A. C. Headlam, is based on the text as provisionally settled by Professors Lock and Sanday.

1. (Jesus saith, Cast out first the beam out of thine own eye), and then shalt thou see to cast out the mote in thy brother's eye.

2. Jesus saith, Except ye fast to the world, ye shall not find the kingdom of God; and unless ye keep the true Sabbath, ye shall not see the Father.

3, 4. Jesus saith, I stood in the midst of the world, and in my flesh I was seen of them, and I found all men drunken, not one found I thirsty among them; and my soul is weary for the sons of men, for they are blind in their heart, and see (not, poor and know not) their poverty.

5. Jesus saith, Wherever there be (two, they are not without) God, and if anywhere there be one, I am with him; raise the stone and there thou shalt find me; cleave the wood, and there am I.

6. Jesus saith, A prophet is not received in his own country, nor doth a physician heal his neighbours.

7. Jesus saith, A city built on the summit of a lofty mountain, and firmly established, cannot fall nor be hidden.

8. Jesus saith, Thou hearest with (one ear), but the other hast thou closed.

Discoveries of this sort bring with them temptation to dwell on their significance, but that must be resisted. There is also temptation to refer to other materials bearing on the history of the Greek alphabet—notably to the inscriptions on the stupendous statue at Abu Simbel, near the second cataract of the Nile—the mere abstract of which would fill this little volume. But the excerpts—varied enough—already given will suffice to indicate what wealth of literature for our knowledge of the past these venerable relics yield, and how poor beyond redemption would the world be if shorn of those records of human thought and feeling, of those grave and gay pictures of life, so closely resembling our own, whereby, too, we learn how superficial have been the changes in human nature throughout the ages of man's tenancy of the earth.

THE DIFFUSION OF THE "PHŒNICIAN" ALPHABET

In the remaining pages the course of the history of the Phœnician alphabet, as we may for convenience still call it, must now be outlined, and for this purpose the following table, an abstract of that given in Canon Isaac Taylor's History of the Alphabet (i. 81), is a convenient guide.

The several alphabets, it will be seen, are grouped under three principal heads: (a) ARAMEAN, whence most of the alphabets of Western Asia are derived; (b) SABÆAN, the source of the alphabets of India; and (c) HELLENIC, the source of the alphabets of Europe.

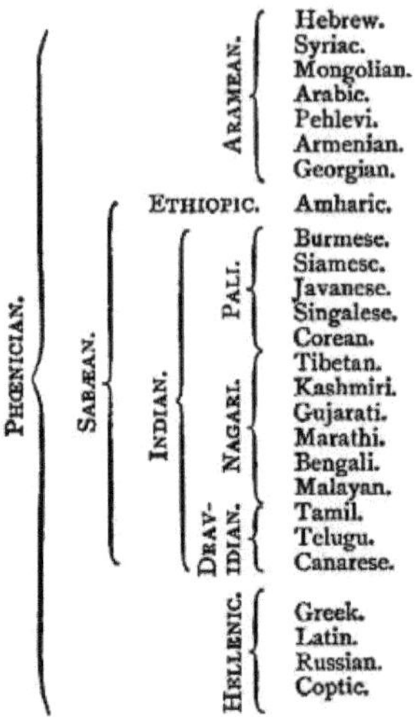

(a) ARAMEAN, so called from "Aram," the hilly district of Mesopotamia, became, from the seventh century B.C., the commercial script of Asia, Aram lying in the line of trade between Egypt and Babylonia. Later on that script was used for official purposes at the Babylonian court, and "ultimately broke up into a number of national alphabets, for which, owing to religious causes, a separate existence became possible. The later alphabets—Parsi, Hebrew, Syriac, Mongolian, and Arabic—were at first local varieties of the Aramean. Owing to accidental circumstances they became the sacred scripts of the five great faiths of Asia—Zoroastrianism, Judaism, Christianity, Northern Buddhism, and Islam. Hence the descendants of the Aramean alphabet occupy a space on the map second only to that filled by the Latin alphabet itself." (Taylor, i. 249.) They are, as indicated in the table: (1) the Hebrew, in whose modern square characters copies of the Scriptures in that language are printed, and the rolls of the Law inscribed; (2) the Syriac, once an important script of Christian literature, but now only in use among some obscure sects; (3) the

Mongolian, which has a curious history, narrated at length in Canon Taylor's volumes (i. pp. 297-312). It is derived from the Syriac, which was carried by Nestorian missionaries throughout Asia. Condemned by the Council of Ephesus in 431 A.D. for certain heresies concerning the dual nature of Christ, these Nestorians fled to Persia, and thence travelling eastward, preached their gospel with such success that the alphabet in which it was written became the dominant script until its supersession by Arabic on the spread of Mohammedanism. (4) The history of Arabic, which is more nearly allied to Syriac than to any other member of the Aramean group, exhibits the aggressive spirit of the Prophet, whose scriptures are transcribed in its beautiful flowing characters. It has exterminated its fellow-Semitic scripts, "expelled the Greek alphabet from Asia Minor, Thrace, Syria, and Egypt, and the Latin alphabet from Northern Africa, and is now used over regions inhabited by more than one hundred millions of the human race." The transactions of the East are recorded in the alphabet of the Koran, so that it would seem, in the world's history, that if "trade follows the flag," the alphabet follows religion.

The so-called "Arabic" numerals are probably of Indian origin, having been brought by Arab traders from the East and introduced by them into Spain in the Middle Ages, whence they spread over Europe, coming into use in England perhaps about the eleventh century. But whether India invented them, or borrowed them from Greek or other traders from the West, is unknown. Counting with the fingers, the most primitive mode of reckoning, and recording by strokes, a method still in vogue, have their limits, and hence (to say nothing of the use of pebbles and beans, and of the abacus) the invention of written signs for the higher numbers; or the adoption of the letters of the alphabet in their order as number-signs, the numerical value increasing with each successive letter; or the use of the initial letter of the word itself for the number. Examples of special symbols for tens, hundreds, and so forth are supplied by Egyptian and Assyrian records, as shown in the following figures:—

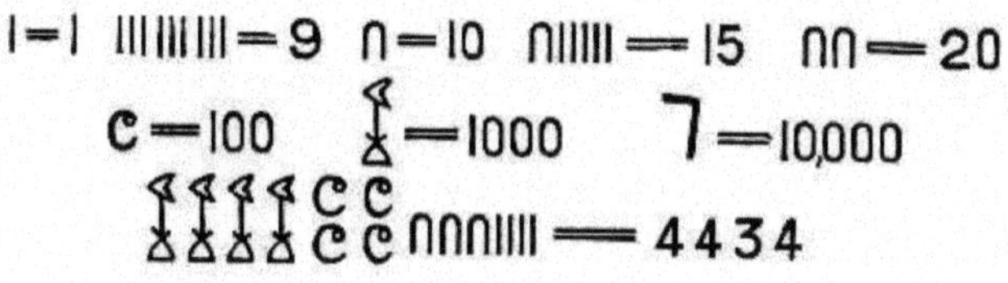

EGYPTIAN NUMERATION

$$\text{Y}=1 \quad \text{<}=10 \quad \text{Y>}=100 \quad \text{<Y>}=(10\times 100)=1000$$

$$\text{YYYY<Y> ᗐ Y> <<<YYYY} = 4434$$

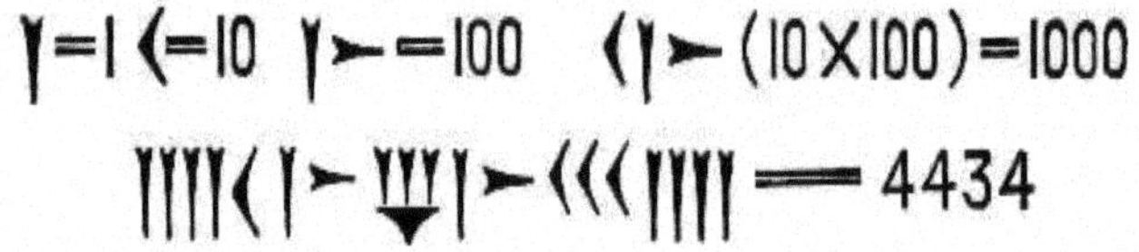

ASSYRIAN NUMERATION

We have examples of the use of letters in their "abecedarian" or acrostic order in the sections of the one hundred and nineteenth and one hundred and forty-fifth Psalms, which bear the letters of the Hebrew alphabet, and in the books of the Iliad, which bear the letters of the Greek alphabet. That alphabet also supplies illustration of the acrologic method, as e.g. Π = Πέντε, for 5; Δ = Δέκα, for 10; H (the old sign for the rough breathing in Ἑκατον), for 100; X = Ξίλιοι, for 1000; Π with Λ (= 5 x 10) inscribed in it standing for 50. A more ingenious method was adopted by both Greeks and Hebrews in the division of the alphabet into three groups: the first to represent units; the second, tens; and the third, hundreds. The use of "Arabic" numerals, besides encountering opposition at the start, was limited until the fifteenth century to the paging of books and mathematical formulæ, but their convenience as compared with the cumbrous Roman figures won them general adoption. Their stages of modification were pictorially suggested by Canon Taylor in a communication to the Academy 28th January 1882, from which the table on p. 212 is borrowed, but the question of origin remains unsettled.

An age to which, more than to its predecessors, with their more sedate lives, "time is money," may appreciate what service they wrought who invented the few numerals, the relative places of which serve the purpose of recording the commerce of the world. But perhaps the greater admiration is due to the genius which devised the nought or cipher (Arab. sifr, "empty"), without which the labour of calculation and recording would have taxed energy beyond endurance.

The (5) Pehlevi, (6) Armenian, and (7) Georgian alphabets are derived from the Aramean group through the Persian or Iranian. The Pehlevi has abiding interest as the script of the sacred books of the Zend or Parsi religion; but the Armenian and Georgian, with the addition of three or four Greek letters, are bereft of significance except as the surviving representatives of the ancient Persian. The Indo-Bactrian alphabet should have reference here as of Iranian descent, and especially because it is the script of the famous edicts of Asoka, the first royal Buddhist convert, inscribed on a rock near Peshawar.

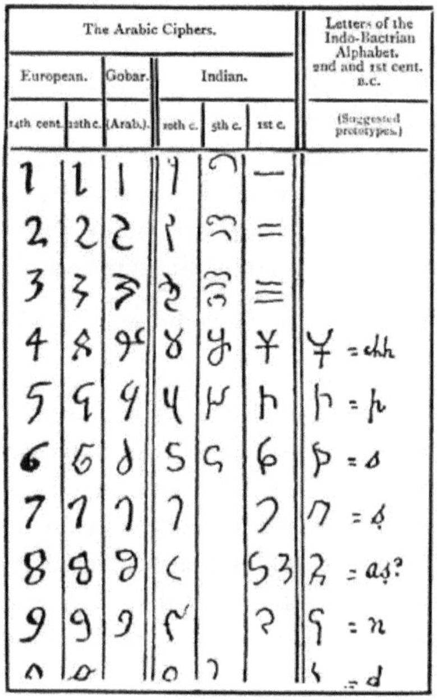
The Arabic Ciphers.
European.
Gobar.
Indian.
14th cent.
12th c.
(Arab.).
10th c.
5th c.
1st c.
Letters of the Indo-Bactrian Alphabet. 2nd and 1st cent. B.C.
(Suggested prototypes.)

(b) THE SABÆAN (from "Sheba") or Himyaritic (from Himyar, the eponymous hero of the Himyarites) group is classed among South Semitic alphabets. The early alphabet of Abyssinia, called Ethiopic or Amharic, is derived from it, and, wherein lies its main importance, also the alphabets of India, the number of which, comprising more than half of the alphabets now in use, would, in detailed treatment, "demand a space wholly disproportionate to any interest which they might possess save to an extremely limited band of specialists." That is Canon Taylor's excuse for passing them over with brevity, and those who care to pursue a subject yielding to few in dryness will find it summarised in the tenth chapter of his work. For the present purpose, the list of alphabets set down in the table will suffice.

(c) THE HELLENIC.—It was a happy chance that, in the westward course of the Phœnician alphabet, the Greeks were the first to receive it. For while the various scripts of Asia and the Malayan Archipelago, which are derived from that alphabet, have retained, in the main, its consonantal character, leaving the vowels to be only partially indicated, the Greeks, with master-touch, shaped it to relative perfection in adding separate letters to represent the vowels, so that there might be a visible sign for every audible sound of the human voice. Besides this, they put some of the superfluous gutturals and sibilants to new uses, simplified other characters, and ultimately transposed the Semitic mode of writing from right to left by writing from left to right. These, and other changes both in the Greek and its derived alphabets, were made slowly and almost imperceptibly, "descent with modification," to apply the Darwinian phrase concerning plants and animals to the scripts of the world, being as much a feature in their history as in that of organisms generally. To complete the parallel, when a certain stage of adaptation is reached, there is, as e.g. in the case of our own alphabet, mainly through the invention of printing, arrest of development. Nature may aim at perfection, but is content with adjustment, and the works of man abide only as they are, in Stoic maxim, "according to nature."

The alphabets derived from the Hellenic are (1) Greek, (2) Russian, (3) Coptic, (4) Latin.

(1) Greek.—To the ancient Greek Hellas meant no defined country, but simply the abode of the Hellenes, whether in Smyrna, Syracuse, Athens, or wherever else they might be found. The mountainous character of Greece explains its division into a crowd of petty states, many of which were no bigger than a modern township. This accorded with Aristotle's view that the area of the state should not be wider than an orator's voice would carry. The physical separation of the peoples explains that political disunion which was the curse of the country from first to last, and accounts for the forty local alphabets which made for discord. But the federation at the time of the Persian invasion, when the victories of Marathon and Salamis fostered conceptions of a common fatherland, was followed by the rise of Athens, and her intellectual supremacy determined that of one of the alphabets. These had settled into two leading groups, the Ionian (in which the Corinthian may be included) and the Chalcidian. The Ionian, which was developed in the famous colony of that name, deviated more from the Phœnician type than the Chalcidian. It was adopted by Athens 483 B.C., and became the classic alphabet of Greece. From it there sprang the Slavonic, Coptic, and other alphabets, while the Chalcidian gave birth to the alphabets of Western Europe.

(2) Russian.—A quaint and probably trustworthy tradition tells how the Greek alphabet was imported into Russia. "Formerly," says John, Exarch of Bulgaria, who wrote in the ninth century, "the Slavonians had no books, but they read and made divinations by means of pictures and figures cut on wood, being pagans. After they had received baptism they were compelled, without any proper rules, to write their Slavonic tongue by means of Greek and Latin letters. But how could they write well in Greek letters such words as Bog, Zhivot, Zelo, or Tserkov, and others like these? And so many years passed by. But then God, loving the human race, had pity on the Slavonians, and sent them St. Constantine, the Philosopher, called Cyril, a just and true man, who made for them an alphabet of thirty-eight letters, of which some were after the Greek style, and some after the Slavonic language." The variety of sounds in Slavonic involved the addition of ten

characters to Cyril's alphabet, and although that number was afterwards reduced, the Russian remains the most cumbersome and ungainly of alphabets.

(3) Coptic, or, more correctly, the Coptic script of Egypt under the Romans. Notwithstanding the advent of Cæsar Augustus as Prefect of Egypt, Greek influence prevailed, and the native Christians, in transcribing the Coptic version of the Bible, used the Greek alphabet, borrowing some half-dozen of the ancient Egyptian demotic signs to express sounds unrepresented by the Greek. But, as throughout Mohammedan countries, Arabic has supplanted Coptic, which is now used only for liturgical purposes, "perhaps little if at all understood by the priests who have to use it in the services of the Church."

(4) Latin.—This is, far and away, the most important of all alphabets. As stated above, it is derived from the Chalcidian type of the Hellenic, so called because in use at Chalcis, in Eubœa, an island of the Ægean, whence migrated one of the several Greek colonies planted in Southern Italy. As the oldest Italic scripts—copying the older method of the Greek—read from right to left, and as the first thing aimed at by the colonists would be the use of common sound-signs and numerals, there is good warrant for fixing the date of the introduction of the Greek alphabet into Italy at about the eighth century before Christ. The various derived scripts—Umbrian, Oscan, Etruscan, and others—have all, the Latin alone excepted, passed away. The ultimate dominance of the Latins brought about the abolition of every other alphabet than their own, which, becoming the alphabet of the Roman Empire, and then of Christendom, secured an everlasting supremacy. It was the vehicle of Greek and Roman culture to Western Europe; it is the vehicle of all the culture of the progressive races of the world. Although essentially identical with the Greek, it took its own line, and that, compared with the Slavonic, a simple one. The earliest Indo-European or "Aryan" language contained, so far as can be discovered, twelve consonants and three vowels (i, a, u), and to these last the Latin added e and o. It at first rejected the Greek K, and used C for the sounds of both k and g, but later on added a bar to the lower end of C, converting it into G. Similarly, R is but a variation of P, by the addition of a stroke below the crook. And while the later Greek rejected Q, the Latin retained it. But not to multiply examples, citations of which are confusing in the absence of explanations of the causes necessitating changes of form, explanations too technical for admission here (see for examples Taylor, ii. 140), it may suffice to give a few specimens of variations between the older and newer Latin and Greek forms.

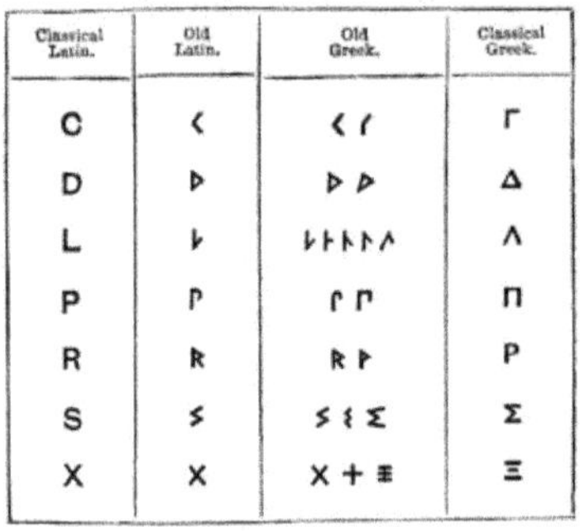
Classical Latin.
Old Latin.
Old Greek.
Classical Greek.
C
D
L
P
R
S
X

FINAL LATIN AND GREEK FORMS COMPARED WITH THEIR PROTOTYPES IN THE OLDER ALPHABETS

In the early empire the Romans used two sorts of characters, Capital and Cursive. The Capitals were square-shaped or rustic, i.e. slightly ornamented. They were used for inscriptions and other writing demanding prominence, as we use capitals nowadays, borrowing the old Roman forms. The Cursive or running characters are the originals of our small types, and were used for correspondence and other purposes where rapid writing was an object, abbreviations, which are the forerunners of our modern "shorthand," being sometimes employed. Out of this cursive hand there arose a variety of hand-writings, the most important among these being the Irish "semi-uncial." The appearance of this script in that island is one of the problems of graphiology. "No Irish hand is known out of which it could have arisen. And yet in the sixth century Ireland suddenly becomes the chief school of Western calligraphy, and the so-called Irish uncial blazes forth in full splendour as the most magnificent of all mediæval scripts. Only one conclusion seems possible. Some time in the fifth century a fully-formed, book-hand must have been introduced by St. Patrick (432-458 A.D.), doubtless from Gaul, where he received his consecration. And this must have been cultivated as a calligraphic script in the Irish monasteries, which at this time enjoyed comparative immunity from the ravages of the Teutonic invaders, who, in the fifth century, desolated Italy, Gaul, and Spain." (Taylor, ii. 173.) Irish monks introduced it into Northumbria, and in course of time there was derived from it the "Caroline minuscule," as it is called, because it was introduced in the reign of Charlemagne in the famous school at Tours founded by Alcuin of York, a celebrated scholar of the eighth century, and friend of the Emperor. As a clear hand, compressible into a small space, it grew rapidly in favour till the end of the twelfth century, when a period of decadence, of which the ugly "Black Letter" was the result, set in and held sway in Western Europe for a generation after the discovery of printing with movable types. The Black-letter characters were imitations of the coarse thick characters of the monkish manuscripts, and it was not till the early part of the sixteenth century that they were displaced in England by the Roman letters, whose basis is the Caroline minuscule (see p.37). Here, however, we are on the threshold of the "chapel," and must retrace our steps for brief survey of the few changes introduced into the Latin alphabet in adapting it to the requirements of the English language. These are shown in the admirable table borrowed from Canon Taylor. (History of the Alphabet, i. 72.) The order of the letters (an unexplained problem in the history of the alphabet) approximates to that of the Phœnicians, and their names are based on the same principle as that of the Latin. Running our eye down the table we note that our alphabet provides for certain phonetic variations by turning the Latin I into I and J, and VV or UV into double U = W. The Anglo-Saxon, which appears to be partly Roman and partly Irish in origin, had borrowed two useful characters from the Runic, Þ = w, named wen, and Þ = th, named thorn, which for a time formed part of the English alphabet. The thorn has been revived of late, as a bastard archaic, in the printing of the as y^e, with consequent mispronunciation of that word by those who see it thus changed. Both Y and Z were late importations from the Greek into the Latin, being used only in Greek loan-words to denote sounds peculiar to the Greek; hence, as the most recent arrivals, their appearance at the end of the alphabet. Some of our letters are of little use; K makes C superfluous, and Q and X are of no more service to us than they were to the Romans. So that, for practical purposes, we have only twenty-three letters wherewith to indicate at least thirty-two sounds. Thus our alphabet, like our spelling (which is ever at war with our pronunciation, to the bewilderment of school children and foreigners), is what it is from the lack of any consistent rule. Nevertheless, so workable a set of signs has secured a footing which, made firmer by the art of printing, is not likely to be disturbed by any processes of phonetic change which mark the course of speech. To that art of printing is also due those modifications in handwriting which distinguish the penmanship of past and present times. As has been seen, while Germany remained in fetters to the eye-distracting Black letter, we freed ourselves by adoption of the clear Roman type; hence the disappearance, save in legal documents and a few show art-books, of the cramped hand which prevailed down to the sixteenth century. So the handwriting of to-day (good, bad, and indifferent, as the personal equation of each one of us shapes it), which we learned at school through the stages of "pot-hooks and hangers" to the grandest flourishes of copy-book "maxims," is derived from the same source as the printed alphabet.

GENEALOGY OF THE ENGLISH ALPHABET.

Old Greek	Euboean	Latin	Uncial	Minuscule	Venetian	Roman
A	A	A	ᴀ	a a	a	a
B	B	B	Bb	b	b	b
Γ	Γ	< C / G	C ҁ Ꝛ	c Ʒ ɡ g	c ɡ	c g
Δ	ᐅ	D	Ɒ ᴆ	ᴆ ᴆ	d	d
Ɛ	Ɛ	E	Є ɘ	e ɛ	e	e
F	F	F	F	f	f	f
I	I	Z	Ꝫ	ʝ	z	z
⊟	H	H	ƕ b	ƕ	h	h
⌇	I	I	J	i j	i j	i j
K	K	K	K	κ ʞ	k	k
⋁	⌐	⌐L	ʟʟ	l	l	l
⋔	M	MM	ɷ	m	m	m
N	N	N	ɴ	n	n	n
Ξ	+	X	Ж	x ɪ	x	x
O	O	O	O	o	o	o
Γ	Γ	P P	P	p	p	p
Φ	Ϙ	Q	ꝗ ꝗ	q	q	q
P	R	R R	R	ɲ r	r	r
Ξ	Ꙅ	ꙅ S	S	ʏ ʃ	ʃ ſ	ſ s
T	T	T	T τ	τ t	t	t
Y	V Y	{ UV Y	u T	u v w y	u v w y	u v w y

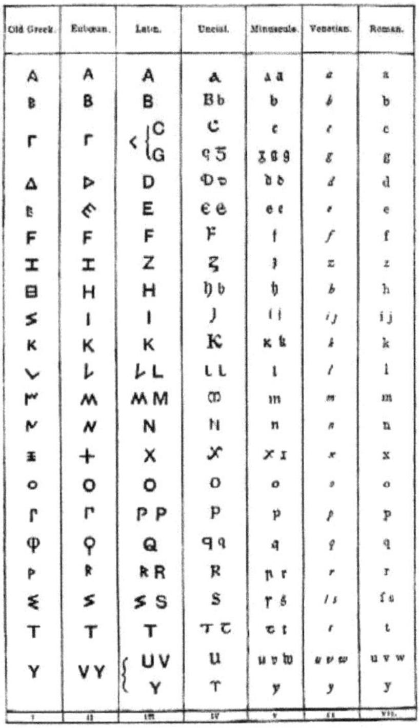

CHAPTER XI
RUNES AND OGAMS

The Runic alphabet originated among the Scandinavians, who probably adapted it from some other script, since no traces of any pictographic characters whence it may have been derived have been found. Some scholars hold that it is derived from the "Phœnician" alphabet; others say that it comes from the Latin. Canon Taylor has a definite theory that it is a degraded form of the Greek alphabet; for in the sixth century B.C. the Goths swarmed in the region south of the Baltic and east of the Vistula, and in their trading relations with Greek colonists north of the Black Sea may readily have obtained a knowledge of the Greek alphabet. The question, however, of origin remains, and is likely to remain, unsettled.

The sharp, angular form of the runes proves that they were incised on wood, stone, or some such rigid material, and these characters persist in the few manuscripts which have been found. The primitive Gothic alphabet is named, on the acrologic principle, "futhorc," after the first six letters, f, u, th, o, r, c. It was divided into three parts or "aetts," named after the first letter of each "aett" or family—"Frey's aett," "Hagl's aett," and "Tyr's aett"—as shown in the following illustration from an article on Runes by Miss Gertrude Rawlings (Knowledge, 1st October, 1896).

RUNE ALPHABET

The Scandinavian, Anglian, and Manx runes are local variants of this oldest form. Runic inscriptions—monumental and sepulchral—have a wide, although exclusive, range. They are found in the valley of the Danube, but not in Germany; in America, but not in Ireland; in the Isle of Man, but not in Wales—thus evidencing their restriction within Scandinavian lines of migration. The oldest was found at Sandwich, in Kent; but an especially interesting example is the well-known Ruthwell Cross in Dumfriesshire, on which is inscribed a poem, "The Dream of the Holy Rood," ascribed to Cædmon, the herdsman poet of the seventh century. The early voyage of the Vikings to Vineland, as they named America, has illustration in a Runic epitaph cut in a rock on the Potomac. "Here lies Syasi, the fair one of Western Iceland, the widow of Koldr, sister of Thorgr, by her father, aged twenty-five years. God be merciful to her." The old alphabet was displaced by the Latin on the conversion of the peoples of Northern Europe to Christianity, but not before Ulphilas, the Bishop of the Goths, had woven some of its characters into the compound script which was the vehicle of his memorable translation of the Gospels, the lovely manuscript of which, in gold and silver letters on purple vellum, is worth a visit to the University of Upsala to see.

The curious Ogam alphabet, which may date from the fifth century A.D., and the use of which did not extend outside the British Isles, is held by some scholars to be derived from the Runic, but its characters indicate that more probably it is a debased copy of the Roman. Ogam, according to Professor Rhys, the highest authority on the subject, probably means "skilled use of words." The letters are formed by straight or slanting strokes drawn above, or beneath, or right through horizontal or perpendicular lines. The alphabet is divided into four aicmes or groups, each containing five letters: the first aicme, B, L, F, S, N being placed under the line (assuming this to be horizontal); the second aicme, H, T, D, C, Qn, above it; the third aicme, M, G, Ng, F(?) R, diagonally through it; and the fourth aicme, comprising the vowels A, O, U, E, I, intersecting it at right angles. Canon Taylor sees in the ogams an adaptation of the runes to the needs of the engraver, "notches cut with a knife on the edge of a squared staff being substituted for the ordinary runes." And he thinks that the derivation of the ogams from runes is shown in the fact that their names agree with the names of runes of corresponding value, and that they are found exclusively in regions where Scandinavian settlements were established. Professor Rhys regards them as "probably, the work of a grammarian acquainted with Roman writing, but too proud to adopt it." The larger number of Ogam inscriptions occur in Ireland; others are scattered over Scotland, Wales, and the south-west of England.

It may be thought that any survey of the history of the Alphabet, however free from overcrowding in detail, and however popular in treatment, would outline the story of the origin of, and changes in, each of the twenty-six letters which are, for the English-speaking races, the vehicle of communication and the depository of knowledge. But, probably, enough has been said to show that the information which would alone warrant such table of derivations is not yet forthcoming, and, perhaps, never will be. The most plausible theory that the wit of man, supported by a set of facts that seemed to hang well together, could devise, was formulated by M. de Rougé, and it has been seen that the epigraphic material found in the Ægean renders his apparently well-based and coherent theory no longer tenable.

Neither would there be advantage in cataloguing the two hundred and fifty alphabets which have come into being since prehistoric man scratched his rude pictographs on the faces of cliffs and on fragments of slate or bone. Some fifty of these alphabets have survived, and of these about half are found in India, but, whatever of historical value they may hold, their use is restricted and local. The rest are, in the main, variations of three scripts—Roman, Arabic, and Chinese—and an outlook on the world's course makes it no matter of doubt that it is with the Roman, as the vehicle of culture of the most advancing races of mankind, that there lies the maintenance of supremacy and the extension of its sway.

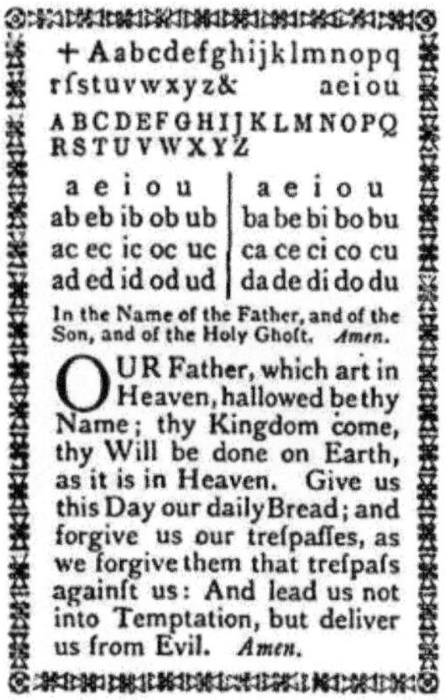

+ Aabcdefghijklmnopq
rſstuvwxyz&　　aeiou
ABCDEFGHIJKLMNOPQ
RSTUVWXYZ

a e i o u	a e i o u
ab eb ib ob ub	ba be bi bo bu
ac ec ic oc uc	ca ce ci co cu
ad ed id od ud	da de di do du

In the Name of the Father, and of the Son, and of the Holy Ghoſt. *Amen.*

OUR Father, which art in Heaven, hallowed be thy Name; thy Kingdom come, thy Will be done on Earth, as it is in Heaven. Give us this Day our daily Bread; and forgive us our treſpaſſes, as we forgive them that treſpaſs againſt us: And lead us not into Temptation, but deliver us from Evil. *Amen.*

HORN BOOK,
ONCE THE UNIVERSAL PRIMER

(Now so excessively rare that a good example fetches £20 and upwards).